100 Most Beautiful Rooms in America

Helen Comstock

100 MOST BEAUTIFUL ROOMS IN AMERICA

REVISED EDITION

BONANZA BOOKS · NEW YORK

DESIGNED BY BRYAN HOLME

Typography by Laurel Wagner

Contents

Foreword

IT HAS NOT BEEN EASY TO SELECT ONLY ONE HUNDRED especially beautiful rooms where antiques are used. There are at the present time very many hundreds of such rooms in existence in America—more, without doubt, than there ever have been. This is in part due to the enlightened restoration of old homes and the building and furnishing of new ones in traditional styles.

Although American antiques predominate in this book, there are many examples of English and French, as well as a few of eighteenth-century Italian. Spanish is also represented, as this type, too, is part of our heritage, though less commonly perpetuated in America today. Around one-third of the rooms shown can be seen by the public, the rest are from private homes. Almost all represent periods beginning with the late seventeenth century and ending with the Victorian, but there is no attempt made to offer here a complete guide to period styles or schools of cabinetmaking. Rather, the purpose of the book is to please the eye with a representative cross section of the best American tradition has to offer in domestic decoration and architecture combined.

Certain conditions have led to the selection. A guiding principle has of course been the claim to authenticity of the furnishings—or, more specifically, the antiques; other factors have been the interesting character of the architecture and its state of preservation, the arrangement of the furniture and its suitability to the room, and the livable atmosphere or charm the whole ensemble creates.

In the interest of space it has also not usually been possible to include more than one or two rooms from the same house. Although others may be equally deserving, a fairly rigorous discipline has had to be followed. The selection as a whole has been further guided to permit the most popular styles of decoration in America to be represented without more stress in one direction or another than is proportionate with the number of existing homes of special type and note.

9

The rooms that may justifiably be considered the most beautiful in America are those that accurately, comfortably, and best reflect today the styles that America has most deeply taken to heart over the centuries. Grandeur and a display of opulence not being a prerequisite of a beautiful room, the selection includes many examples of simple, early styles that are more popular today than they ever were, represented by Time Stone Farm in Marlboro, Massachusetts, and by Ogden House in Fairfield, Connecticut. Of a still earlier period, and more sophisticated in their interpretation of styles typical of late seventeenth-century England, are the pre-Queen Anne interiors of West Saint Marys Manor at Drayden, Maryland, and the home of Mrs. Katharine Prentis Murphy, Guilford, Connecticut. As the eighteenth century advanced there was an increasing awareness of the developing mid-Georgian style; but also a persistent devotion to Queen Anne, which Colonial builders and furniture makers retained in American design well past 1750, as seen at Wilton in Virginia and the Van Cortlandt house in New York. Georgian, represented by Chippendale in furniture, and by the designs of Ware and Langley in architecture, played a dominant role just prior to the Revolution, witnessed by Mount Pleasant in Philadelphia and the Jeremiah Lee Mansion at Marblehead. This same period is of dominant interest in today's homes, as seen at Mount Cuba, Greenville, Delaware, and in the home of Mitchel Taradash at Ardsley-on-Hudson, which are furnished with the finest examples of American cabinetmaking, showing the individuality with which cabinetmakers of Philadelphia, New England, and New York made use of English design. The English source, the handsome and urbane productions of London's craftsmen, is seen at Boxwood in Atlanta, Georgia, and at the home of Charles Blyth in Burlingame, California, as well as at Bonnie Doon, the former South Carolina home of the famous philatelist, Alfred H. Caspary.

Robert Adam's influence in creating the neoclassic style in England spread to America in the Federal period and, while it affected the entire Atlantic coast, has particularly fine representation in the North at Salem, Massachusetts, where, around 1800, Samuel McIntire built homes and carved furniture for prosperous shipowners; and in the South at Charleston, South Carolina, where a number of older houses were remodeled in the Adam style about the same time. The Peirce-Nichols and Pingree houses in Salem, which are open to the public, are furnished chiefly with McIntire pieces; but in the Charleston houses, still in private hands, their owners have shown the successful results of mingling many styles, frequently including French Louis XV and Louis XVI pieces with Chippendale, Adam, and Sheraton.

The Greek Revival in architecture, with America's interpretation of a new wave of classic influence in the early nineteenth century, produced Andalusia, near Philadelphia, and Bartow, near New York, their furnishings combining influences of the late Empire in France and the Regency in England. Serving as a prelude to the Victorian, the most eclectic of all styles, there is Arlington, near Natchez, Mississippi, where the Victorian of the Louis Philippe period recapitulates that of Louis XV. Frill upon frill was added by the later Victorians. John Belter of New York sent his heavily carved furniture to many parts of the country; and Belle Meade, near Nashville, Tennessee, preserves some of his work.

French furniture has exerted an influence in America from the eighteenth century—witness the Philadelphia-made chairs at Lemon Hill—and in our time has its devoted collectors. The Frick Mansion in New York has superb Fragonard and Boucher rooms, furnished with masterpieces by the *maîtres ébénistes* of the reigns of Louis XV and Louis XVI which display the elegance and purity of form that the French craftsmen had at their command. The blend of formality and intimacy that can be achieved with French furniture is seen in a modern house at Huntington Palisades, Los Angeles. French furniture of the earlier periods has proved itself a perfect background for Impressionist paintings, strikingly evident in one of the most fascinating rooms in Philadelphia, the salon in the home of Henry P. McIlhenny where paintings by Renoir and Toulouse-Lautrec hang in an Empire setting.

All of the historic styles that have influenced America are superbly demonstrated on the following pages, in rooms that exist in our town and country houses standing today in major historic areas from New England to California. Details in some of them may have changed—this being the privilege and delight of owners—and change of ownership has in some instances taken place, so it cannot be guaranteed that the photographs of these rooms, which have been collected over a period of years, are still accurate to every last detail. They are no less interesting or significant for this reason.

While the Victorian is the latest period style represented, Victorian rooms do not conclude the book. The eight rooms which are shown last recapitulate earlier styles—Louis XV, Louis XVI, Chippendale, Adam, Hepplewhite—in houses remodeled or recently built, and all share a subtly modern feeling. The antiques which furnish them do not differ from those illustrated in the rest of the book. The creators of these rooms have made an asset of modernity while showing appreciation of tradition. They make a fitting conclusion to a book concerned throughout with modern taste in the use of antiques.

For this new edition, the book has been revised to include. Sotterley, Hollywood, St. Marys County, Maryland; a French house in California, home of William C. Kennedy; Boscobel, Garrison-on-Hudson, New York; Van Cortlandt Manor, Croton-on-Hudson, New York; and Hammond-Harwood House, Annapolis, Maryland.

Those who live with their collections have many incentives to study the crafts and skills of the past. For them, and for the student in general, the trail leads on and on, from the arts to broader backgrounds of life in historic epochs. I hope that the reader may feel the attraction of exploring further some of the vistas which are suggested by these interiors whose creators have shown so fine an understanding of the arts of the past.

My appreciation for help at every stage, as well as for the original suggestion for this book, are given with gratitude to Bryan Holme of Studio Books, The Viking Press.

—HELEN COMSTOCK

February 1964

TIME STONE FARM
Marlborough, Massachusetts
HOME OF MRS. ARTHUR M. GREENWOOD

THE GREAT ROOM

An old New England farmhouse built in 1702 by John Goodale and added to over the years by his descendants. It was acquired in 1925 by Dr. and Mrs. Arthur M. Greenwood and restored under the guidance of a well-known student of New England architecture, George Francis Dow. They brought to the house a great collection of American antiques, and after Dr. Greenwood's death in 1947 many pieces were presented to the Smithsonian Institution. The Greenwoods had much affection for the homely objects of everyday life, as may be seen here in the Great Room.

Photographs: Samuel Chamberlain

12

The exposed oak beams and sheathing have the mellow color and texture that only age can give. Here was a room for living, cooking, and dining; and after the meal was prepared at the big fireplace it was eaten at just such a trestle table.

There are without doubt more large, turned armchairs here than the original owner could have possessed, but they belong to his, and his father's, day. At one side is a smaller fireplace, built, tradition says, for a member of the family who refused to associate with the rest. This fireplace is shown at top of the opposite page.

THE IRONMASTER'S HOUSE

Saugus, Massachusetts

THE FIRST IRONWORKS ASSOCIATION

THE KEEPING ROOM

This house, built between 1636 and 1642, was once the home of the ironmaster of Saugus, Richard Leader. He was in charge of the first successful iron refinery and rolling mill in the colonies. It is a splendid example of the early domestic interior of post-and-beam construction with chamfered summer beam and a ten-foot fireplace.

The seventeenth-century gate-leg table is covered appropriately by a Turkey work carpet, a highly prized form of needlework inspired by Near Eastern rugs. The carved great chair with wainscot back, dated 1660, was for the master of a house

14

or an honored guest. A great paneled press cupboard represents a type made in the region, quite likely at Ipswich. There are iron pots, tongs, and racks at the fireplace; a fireback of 1655 from Kittery, Maine; and a spit that was rotated by wheel and chain.

The exterior represents one of the finest surviving examples of early architecture, with steep roof, many gables, clustered chimney, casement windows, and the overhanging second story which, contrary to a widespread notion, was not for defense against the Indians but followed English precedent.

Photographs: Samuel Chamberlain

BUTTOLPH-WILLIAMS HOUSE 1692

Wethersfield, Connecticut

CONNECTICUT ANTIQUARIAN AND LANDMARKS SOCIETY

THE SOUTH CHAMBER

The fireplace in this room, with its bolection molding at the opening and a fielded panel above the mantel shelf, was found intact under plaster when the house was restored in 1947. The paneled door beside it, with tulip hinges, and the great beams

Photographs: Meyers Studio

are original. Grouped three-light casement windows were restored on the precedent of the seventeenth-century English cottage; the original studs for them were found beneath the nineteenth-century sash windows.

The bedroom was recently furnished with gifts from Mrs. Katharine Prentis Murphy. The bed has a valance of flamestitch embroidery and hangings of hand-woven wool. A typical Connecticut paneled chest decorated with split spindles stands under the windows; and the armchair with carved crest has a banister back, the flat sides of the banisters considerably turned to the sitter's back. The heart-and-crown armchair, in the other view, was made in Connecticut, and is painted black and scarlet. The delftware charger on the mantel shows a portrait of William III.

17

HOUSE IN CONNECTICUT
Guilford

HOME OF MRS. KATHARINE PRENTIS MURPHY

THE COTTAGE

Represented in this cottage near Mrs. Murphy's main house at Guilford is what may be called the first period of American furniture—mid-seventeenth century to about 1725—antedating the more familiar Queen Anne and Chippendale.

The New England press cupboard behind the long stretcher table (below) could only have been made for a family of wealth. The tall chest of drawers at the end of the room (below, left), originating in Connecticut, has a stepped top which was

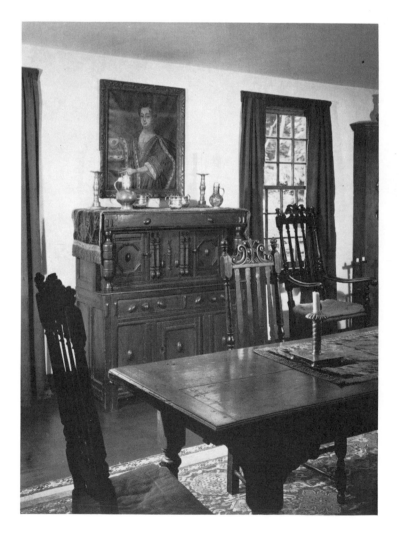

Photographs: Gottscho-Schleisner

intended for the display of fine pieces of silver or delftware. This pottery, so highly esteemed in the late seventeenth century and early eighteenth, was made in Holland and England. A delftware posset pot, used for a drink of hot milk curdled with spiced wine, stands on the chest, and with it, delft plates showing royal portraits.

Mrs. Murphy has recently made generous gifts from her house to the New-York Historical Society and elsewhere.

PHILIPSBURG MANOR, UPPER MILLS ("PHILIPSE CASTLE")

Irvington, New York

SLEEPY HOLLOW RESTORATIONS

THE FORE ROOM

The term "fore room" or "fore parlor" describing one of the chief ground-floor rooms of a house was in use in the early eighteenth century.

These furnishings, brought during the course of restoration to the late seventeenth-century Dutch New York house of the first lord of the manor of Philipsburg, Frederick Philipse, give an impression of the substantial wealth of a successful merchant. His ships, trading with Holland and, no doubt, the West Indies, were loaded and unloaded at this spot on the Pocantico River. They brought back wares that were sold to the surrounding region. Frederick Philipse was a frequent patron of New York silversmiths, a further indication of his prosperity. He could well have owned the fine melon-bulb draw-table, lacquer cabinet, handsome brass candlesticks and andirons, and the other objects appropriately displayed here.

The patent for this manor was granted in 1693; lands extended from the Hudson to the Bronx River, and from the Haarlem River to Croton. After the death of

Philipse in 1702 the manor was divided and this part of his estate, which was known as the "Upper Mills," passed to his son, Adolph. The other part was administered from the Philipse Manor House at Yonkers. After 1785 the house at Upper Mills became known as "Philipse Castle," and this obviously inappropriate name has persisted. However, the recent discovery of the designation "Upper Mills," in records as early as 1700, has reinstated the original form.

The portrait of Marÿa Vollenhoven by W. S. de Gust the Elder, which hangs in the corner of the room, represents the type of seventeenth-century Dutch portrait that influenced the work of Hudson Valley portrait painters.

Photographs: Richard Averill Smith

WEST ST. MARYS MANOR

St. Marys County, Maryland

HOME OF COLONEL AND MRS. MIODRAG R. BLAGOJEVICH

Photographs: Richard W. Bohnke

THE DINING ROOM

Jacobean and late Stuart styles dominate this dining room in a small Southern country house built around 1690 on the first grant of land in Maryland. The land was given as reward to Captain Henry Fleet for his aid in establishing the first settlement in the province.

Colonel and Mrs. Blagojevich have restored the house and gathered here a choice collection of seventeenth-century furnishings. This type of furniture possesses far more livable qualities than are usually credited to it. The New England paneled press cupboard of oak, paneled chest of drawers, and turned chairs of Carver type are all seventeenth-century pieces.

Blue and white delftware, brass candlesticks, an early eighteenth-century English brass chandelier, framed stumpwork embroidery, a brass lantern clock on a wall bracket, and the silk flamestitch table cover embroidered on a beige ground with pastel colorings give additional character and impart a glowing warmth to the whole room. A portrait of Charles I hangs above the press cupboard.

THE MISSION HOUSE 1739
Stockbridge, Massachusetts

Photographs: Samuel Chamberlain

THE PARLOR

For nearly two hundred years the Mission House stood on Prospect Hill in need of rescue. Then, in 1929, Miss Mabel Choate purchased it, moved it to the center of Stockbridge, and restored it as a memorial to her father and mother, Mr. and Mrs. Joseph H. Choate.

Wood paneling such as this is remarkable in a frontier settlement, which is what Stockbridge was at the time the house was erected. John Sergeant, missionary to the Housatonic Indians, built the house in 1739 for his bride, Abigail Williams, sister of Ephraim Williams, founder of Williams College. Sergeant, a Yale graduate of 1729, was appointed missionary in 1734.

It is obvious from the paneling and doorway of Connecticut Valley type that some workman from the central part of Massachusetts must have found his way to the Berkshires. Miss Choate has furnished the parlor with unpretentious pieces: a plain Queen Anne highboy, a desk-on-frame, and early Queen Anne side chairs of Dutch type with straight backs. A touch of elegance, such as might be expected in the environment of Abigail Williams, is the Queen Anne easy chair covered in fine eighteenth-century crewelwork. Facing it across the fireplace is an excellent Carver chair, named from one of this type belonging to John Carver, first governor of Plymouth Plantation.

Photographs: Gottscho-Schleisner

CONNECTICUT SALT BOX

Guilford, Connecticut

HOME OF THE MISSES ELIZABETH
AND AGNES DOWNS

THE LIVING ROOM

This is the "keeping room" of early days: the ground floor area that served as a kitchen, dining room, living room, and sometimes a bedroom.

The house, built in 1723, was restored by the late Joseph Downs in 1936, when he was curator of the American Wing of the Metropolitan Museum. The great beams and posts and the lintel of the nine-foot fireplace are of hewn oak; the sheathing of the wall is poplar. In the back wall of the fireplace is a beehive oven. This is lined with stone instead of brick, which is an unusual construction, though other examples are known in the region.

In general, the furnishings are chiefly of the early eighteenth century. Little throughout the entire house can be dated later than Queen Anne. A typical "sparking bench" is seen against the newel post at the staircase, and a fine early slat-back armchair stands near the fireplace. In the view shown above, the Connecticut paneled chest near the window is of the type made in the vicinity of Hartford.

27

MARLPIT HALL
Middletown, New Jersey
MONMOUTH COUNTY HISTORICAL ASSOCIATION

Photographs: Gottscho-Schleisner

THE PARLOR

There is a combination of New England and Dutch influence in this early eighteenth-century New Jersey house, which takes its picturesque name from local deposits of marl, which had economic value in the early days. Over forty years ago, when King's Highway was widened, the house was saved from destruction by being moved.

The original house of 1684 was enlarged between 1720 and 1750, and the paneled parlor is a good example of the mid-eighteenth century. The woodwork is painted a greenish blue. The coat-of-arms of Taylor, over the fireplace, represents George and Helena Taylor, who were living in the house in 1710. The furniture, brought to the house at the time of its restoration in 1933, was practically all found locally, including the Pennsylvania lowboy, a Queen Anne dropleaf table, and small pedestal table. The tall clock is by a Monmouth County maker; and the lady shown in the portrait, Phoebe Hann Vanderhoef, is said to have been its first owner.

THE WILLIAM TRENT HOUSE
Trenton, New Jersey
THE TRENT HOUSE ASSOCIATION

Photographs: Frank May, Jr.

THE PARLOR

While the furnishings were being acquired for this house during its restoration in 1934-1936, frequent reference was made to an inventory of William Trent's estate, taken in 1726.

The house, built as a country mansion on the Delaware by Judge William Trent of Philadelphia, became the center of "Trent Town," as he named the township. In its later history the building was occupied by Washington's assistant quartermaster general and three governors of New Jersey. Additions made during the Victorian period had all but engulfed the old house. However, when its restoration was undertaken, original paneling was found under papered walls, and its great arched stair hall was intact.

Mention in the inventory of a tea table japanned in gold, and of a japanned corner cupboard, led to the acquisition of the attractive group for the parlor shown opposite. The little Queen Anne lacquered tea table and hanging cabinet, around which three late seventeenth-century caned side chairs are drawn up, makes a perfect setting for tea. Since William Trent built his house in 1719, furnishings of the time have been carefully chosen. The latest pieces are of Queen Anne style; there is no Georgian or Chippendale influence such as we find in so many historic colonial houses. In purity of style the Trent House is unsurpassed.

THE PRENTIS HOUSE

Shelburne Museum, Shelburne, Vermont

THE PARLOR

That rich color was known in the homes of Puritan New England may not be too generally realized. Warmth and color were given an interior by such objects as we see here—chairs covered in flamestitch embroidery, lacquered furniture, shining brasses, and painted woodwork.

The house, a 1730 salt box from Hadley, Massachusetts, was acquired by Mrs. J. Watson Webb and moved to the village museum created by her at Shelburne. It was erected there in 1955.

Photograph: Taylor & Dull; courtesy of Antiques

Mrs. Katharine Prentis Murphy presented the furnishings, and the house was opened in 1957. The rare collection of New England furniture, fine old embroideries, fabrics, and lighting devices makes the house a veritable museum of the decorative arts for the period 1690-1750.

MOWBRA HALL

Scarsdale, New York

HOME OF MR. AND MRS. RALPH E. CARPENTER, JR.

THE PHILLIPS PARLOR

This room from the Christopher Phillips house at Wickford, Rhode Island, once known as "Mowbra Castle," represents an early and popular type of wall decoration in New England in which paneling was painted to imitate wood grain. Examples of the so-called "cedar rose graining" survive in old houses, but seldom does a whole room retain its original treatment, let alone in this excellent state of preservation.

The Phillips house, built in 1707, was enlarged around 1745, which is the probable date of the parlor in its present form. In the hall adjoining the parlor, the olive-green shade of the woodwork represents the taste of the eighteenth century for pronounced color. The plaster walls are white. This hall came from a house built by Caleb Mills about 1750 in Medford, Massachusetts, and is one of a series of eighteenth-century rooms taken from houses that were torn down to make way for business structures and which have now been brought together in the home recently built by Mr. and Mrs. Carpenter at Scarsdale.

Photographs: Harold Haliday Costain; courtesy Antiques

THE OGDEN HOUSE
Fairfield, Connecticut
HOME OF MISS MARY ALLIS

THE LONG ROOM

In the salt-box end of the Ogden House the long room with its great fireplace was the center of family life in the eighteenth century. This is not actually the earliest portion of the house, which was built by Richard Ogden around 1690. Additions were made in 1715-1720; and the lean-to, of which this is a part, was added about 1740.

The stone-lined fireplace was used for cooking in the early days, and the kitchen was also the living room. Today this is the living room still, but a new kitchen exists in the comfortably restored house.

To embellish the room Miss Allis has sought examples of furniture that collectors now place in a classification of its own—"Country Furniture." This simple type is appreciated because of its livable qualities and good New England craftsmanship.

Warm touches of color are given to the room by the patterned rugs, curtains and upholstered furniture set off against the white walls, natural wood and stone background.

The exterior of the house, weathered to a dark brown, has original old shingles three feet long, overlapped twice with twelve inches exposed, an eighteenth-century form of insulation which can be admired and envied today.

STRATFORD HALL 1725-1730
Westmoreland County, Virginia
THE ROBERT E. LEE MEMORIAL FOUNDATION

Photographs: James R. Dunlop

THE GREAT HALL

The Great Hall at Stratford is entered directly from outside by two flights of balustraded stone steps, centrally placed on each front. The great clustered chimneys joined by arches shelter a platform from which the builder of the house, Thomas Lee, could see his ships approaching a mile away, on the Potomac.

Lee was of the third generation of his family in America, active in affairs of the colony. In 1722 he married Hannah, daughter of the wealthy Philip Ludwell. About 1725 he began to build his house, which is of the old Tudor H-shape but has classic interior design, as in English houses of the early eighteenth century. This would indicate that Lee was conversant with the new Palladian style.

The Great Hall was a formal room for dancing and entertaining and was kept bare of furniture. Portraits of the Lees hang here. Shown is Arthur, "the diplomat," son of Thomas. He and his brothers, Richard Henry and Francis Lightfoot, Signers of the Declaration of Independence, were born at Stratford. It was also the birthplace of their kinsman, Robert E. Lee.

By 1929, when restoration by the Robert E. Lee Memorial Foundation began, little was left of the former grandeur of Stratford save the impressive woodwork and its exterior. The Great Hall, the finest early paneled room in America, has been painted its original color, a blue-gray. The curtains are of antique red damask.

38

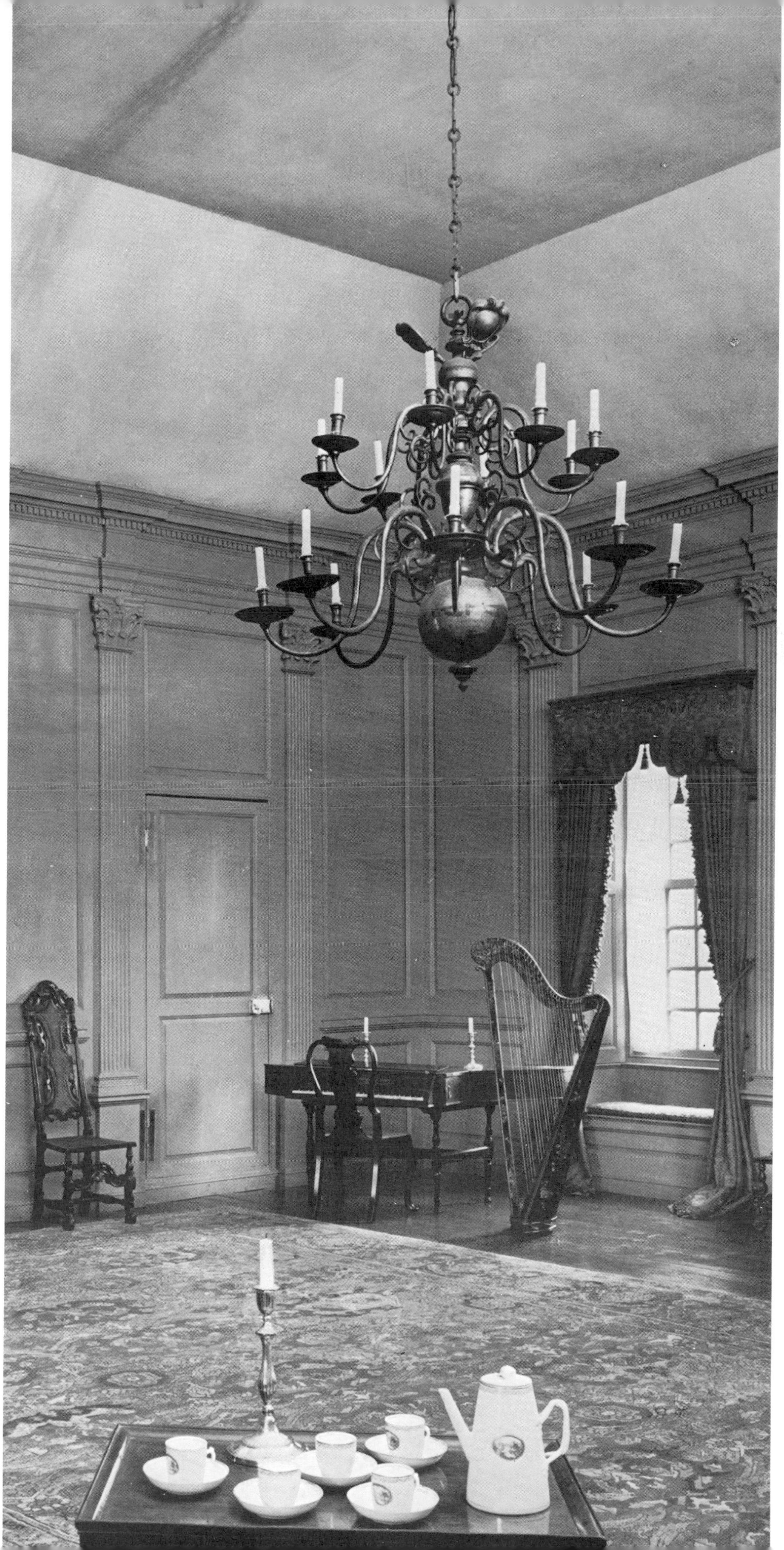

WILTON
Richmond, Virginia
THE SOCIETY OF COLONIAL DAMES OF
AMERICA IN THE STATE OF VIRGINIA

Photographs: Dementi

THE NORTHWEST PARLOR

An inscribed date, 1753, the record of a workman as he finished a cornice, gives a definite year for the completion of Wilton. It is not only rare for this inscribed date but also because it is the only house of the period in which all rooms, halls, closets, and recesses are paneled from floor to ceiling. This paneling, although of the mid-eighteenth century, is such as Sir Christopher Wren favored at its beginning. In the colonies styles, of course, lingered.

The white Carrara marble facing of the fireplace in the northwest parlor is flush with the paneling above it, and its keystone is carved to match those in the arches. Over the fireplace is Wollaston's portrait of William Randolph III, for whom Wilton was built—six miles below Richmond on the James River. This is one of ten family

portraits, including that of William's granddaughter, Elizabeth, which were original to the house and have been lent by the Virginia Historical Society.

The house was rescued from destruction in 1933 by the Colonial Dames and moved to its present site in the residential part of Richmond, still on the James River. The Garden Club of Virginia built its terraced garden leading down to the old canal, and the box at the entrance already gives the impression of age.

An inventory taken in 1810 aided in the selection of furniture for the house, and its placing in the different rooms. The original wall colorings were found under layers of paint, and this room was restored to a deep cream color.

Among the outstanding pieces are the Queen Anne easy chair and the pair of fine Philadelphia side chairs at the piecrust tea table set with Chinese "Lowestoft." The damask draperies are red; this color being repeated in the covering of the sofa. The two large armchairs are upholstered in gold-yellow damask.

THE PARLOR

The house occupied by the Reverend Jonathan Ashley at Deerfield from 1732 to 1780 has a scroll-pedimented doorway. This is distinctive of the Connecticut Valley and of a number of early Deerfield houses.

Photographs: Samuel Chamberlain

THE PARSON ASHLEY HOUSE
Deerfield, Massachusetts
HERITAGE FOUNDATION

The outstanding piece in the parlor is a Massachusetts secretary (opposite) with unusual pierced gilt finials. It was made about 1770, probably by Benjamin Frothingham of Charlestown, now a part of Boston. The first owner was John Marsh, a chaplain in Washington's army. Later the secretary belonged to Longfellow and was used in his house at Cambridge before passing to his son-in-law, Richard Henry Dana, who wrote *Two Years Before the Mast*.

Photograph: Taylor & Dull

The slate blue paneling in this room had to be restored; and the design of the shell cupboards, painted buttermilk red, at the fireplace was patterned exactly on an existing eighteenth-century cupboard from the Williams House in Deerfield, a cupboard which is now at Memorial Hall.

The New England Queen Anne armchair at the fireplace is covered in early needlework in tones of blue, old red, and tan, one of many examples of early embroidery that abound in Deerfield houses.

THE LINDENS
Washington, D.C.

HOME OF MRS. GEORGE MAURICE MORRIS

Photographs: Cortlandt V. D. Hubbard

44

THE BLUE BEDROOM

The Blue Bedroom contains many treasures of English needlework. Crewelwork of the Charles II period hangs at the window and dresses the Queen Anne bed. Over the fireplace Charles II embroidery is seen in a framed panel on the light blue wood-work, and a stumpwork box of unusual size stands on the ball-foot chest of drawers against the white wall by the door. A Cromwellian chair next to it has its original Turkey-work covering.

The Lindens, one of the great mid-Georgian mansions of Massachusetts, was built at Danvers by the wealthy merchant "King" Hooper of Marblehead. In 1935 it was moved to Washington, an unusually long trek even in this day when many old houses are moved from their original sites. The Lindens is three stories high, with roof balustrade, cornice modillions, corner quoins, and two-story columns flanking the main entrance.

The view from the doorway of the Blue Bedroom shows the Dufour wallpaper which continues down the stairwell to the entrance hall. This, illustrating the *Voyage of Antenor* and other motifs in bright blue, greens, and other colors, is original to the house and was probably hung about 1830.

45

Photographs: Gottscho-Schleisner

THE LIVING ROOM

There is not a piece in this room that would not add luster to a museum collection. To select the most important examples is difficult, but the New England kettle-base secretary should certainly be named among them. It was made for the Banning family of Newport, probably in Boston or its vicinity, where the construction of the bombé or kettle-base was fully mastered.

The New York Sheraton sofa has the back rail superbly carved with "thunderbolts" and drapery swags in a manner which proclaims it the work of Duncan Phyfe. The New York tea table, with unusual double-beaded molding, belonged originally to the Pearsall family of New York. Its square-cut claw and ball is typical of New York work.

Where most collectors would count themselves fortunate to have one fine Bilbao mirror, this house has two pairs, one at the door of the living room, the other (shown) hanging over two Philadelphia lowboys.

The walls of the room are gray-green, the mantel, window frames, and cornice, antique white. Silk damask draperies have a design of pale gold and amethyst on faded green. A light gold damask is used on the Philadelphia Chippendale sofa and the one by Duncan Phyfe is covered in antique raspberry satin.

47

MOUNT VERNON
Fairfax County, Virginia
MOUNT VERNON LADIES' ASSOCIATION

THE WEST PARLOR

Before Washington built his "new" room in 1786 the West Parlor was the room for formal entertaining. It was completed in 1759 during his extensive remodeling of Mount Vernon at the time of his marriage to Martha Parke Custis.

The room now contains many pieces original to the house. This is due to the unremitting labor of the Mount Vernon Ladies' Association which, since 1853, has been trying to bring back to Mount Vernon its widely scattered furnishings. Many pieces had been willed by Martha Washington to members of the Custis family.

Among Washington's own pieces are the English card table and the Sheffield Argand lamps standing on it. Also his are the porcelain tea set and the silver tray

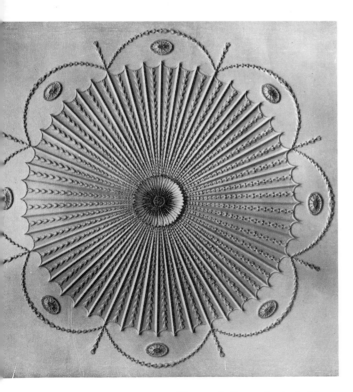

otographs: James R. Dunlop

on which it stands, the latter made for him by Ephraim Brasher of New York. One of the Louis XVI French armchairs at the fireplace was his, and the other comes from the Château de Chavagniac, where Lafayette was born. The fireback shows initials, G W, surmounted by the Washington crest. His arms and crest are on the cartouche above the fireplace, and appear again on the Adam mirror between the windows.

The stucco ceilings here (see detail photo opposite) and in the dining room are among the finest in America, being surpassed only by those at Kenmore and done by the same workman, who was probably French. His name is unknown but he is frequently mentioned as the "stucco man" in the correspondence of Lund Washington, who supervised the work after Washington's departure in 1775.

The wood paneling is white, the armchairs are upholstered in an antique yellow damask matching the draperies, and the design of the carpet is in soft shades of yellow, white and green on a black background.

49

THE WEST CHAMBER

The use of a lowboy in its original function as a dressing table is seen in this room. The other details of furniture arrangement and types of lighting devices show a careful study of pre-Queen Anne as well as mid-eighteenth-century American decoration. The setting is in the same 1730 house as the room reproduced on page 33, but this room represents a slightly later date than the parlor.

When Mrs. J. Watson Webb restored the house, the beams were painted the bright colors that made the homes of our ancestors so inviting. Noteworthy here are the bedhangings of crewelwork on linen, done in New England about 1750. The widely-spaced floral design is typical of American work, but seldom is so large an example seen. The quilted bedspread is of a forgotten fabric called "say," a mixture of wool and silk.

The charming portrait of a little girl in red, over the fireplace, repeats in higher key some of the tones in the hangings. This room, like the rest of the house, has been furnished by Mrs. Katharine Prentis Murphy.

Photograph: Taylor & Dull; courtesy of Antiques

Photographs: Thomas L. Williams, Colonial Williamsburg

BRUSH-EVERARD HOUSE
Williamsburg, Virginia
COLONIAL WILLIAMSBURG

THE PARLOR

The eighteenth-century material for the brilliant red moreen draperies which gave such distinction to this parlor was found on a Virginia plantation. It is so fresh in appearance it seems impossible that this fabric with watered design (impressed by hot irons) is two centuries old. The pattern of the valances is taken from an original eighteenth-century valance.

The Brush-Everard house was one of Williamsburg's comparatively few permanent residences, since the planters came to the capital only at "public times." It is furnished as it might have appeared not long after the middle of the eighteenth century, with Queen Anne and Chippendale pieces, an eighteenth-century landscape as an overmantel painting, and an attractive tea equipage of porcelain.

William Dering, a Williamsburg portrait painter, once lived here; the portrait of Elizabeth Stith which hangs in this room over a Philadelphia sofa is his work. The names of the artist and subject of the portrait of a little girl are unknown but her costume makes her at home in this Colonial Williamsburg setting.

53

THE GOVERNOR'S PALACE
Williamsburg, Virginia

THE PARLOR

A residence for the royal governors of Virginia was begun in 1720 and, because the completion of it was costly, the building came to be called the "Palace." Seven royal governors occupied it, the last being the Earl of Dunmore, who fled in 1775, and whose statement of losses in the London Record Office provided a long list of his furniture that proved helpful in suggesting the present furnishings.

Reconstruction of the Palace was begun in 1930. The original building had been burned in 1781, but foundation walls still existed, and there was a floor plan made by Thomas Jefferson in 1779 when he occupied the Palace as the second governor of the Commonwealth of Virginia. A plan of the position of the outbuildings and outlines of the grounds appeared on a military map drawn in 1782 by a French cartographer. Most important of all, there was a view of the exterior, the only eighteenth-century view so far discovered, on an engraved copperplate in the Bodleian Library, Oxford. On the basis of all this evidence, the Palace has been re-created and furnished as it might have appeared between 1751, when the ballroom wing was added, and the departure of Dunmore. Furnishings are largely English throughout the Palace and its dependencies but there are also New England and Philadelphia pieces and a few of Southern origin, representing styles from the late seventeenth century through the Queen Anne and Chippendale periods.

These recent views of the small parlor opening off the entrance hall show a table with tea equipage before an antique white and brown marble mantel on which is arranged a group of colorful Chelsea porcelain birds with the raised red anchor and anchor marks. The portrait above them, which portrays the beautiful Evelyn Byrd, daughter of William Byrd II of Westover, shows her in a blue gown, against a blue sky with pink-tinged clouds. The English George II chair is covered in antique needlework in red, yellow, blue, green, and gray on a brown ground. The settee and side chairs are covered in gold damask. Curtains are of the same tone but of rare eighteenth-century fabric. The English needlework carpet has a yellow ground, with green border. Both show a floral design in naturalistic colors.

Photographs: George Beamish

TRYON PALACE
New Bern, North Carolina
TRYON PALACE COMMISSION

THE UPSTAIRS SITTING ROOM

Work on the reconstruction of the residence of the royal governors of North Carolina was started in 1952 under the direction of the Tryon Palace Commission, an organization created by the state of North Carolina in 1945. The undertaking, now brought to a fruitful conclusion, had its origin in funds generously provided by Mrs. James Edward Latham.

The original building, of which only the west wing survived to the present, was built after Governor William Tryon arrived from London in 1764 to find that he had no residence, and the colony no fixed capital. John Hawks, an English builder who came over on the same ship, made the plans, based on Plate X of Robert Morris' *Select Architecture,* and sent for workmen from Philadelphia and metalworkers from England. In 1770 Tryon moved his own luxurious personal effects into a residence called one of the handsomest in colonial America, but he did not enjoy it long. He was sent almost immediately to be governor of New York and took his

Bayhall, Kent. *Seat of the Amherst family. By Jan Siberechts; c.1680. This type of architecture inspired Colonial builders. The picture hangs over the fireplace.*

Entrance doorway, carved over-door panel with polychromed Royal Arms of George III. Engraved brass lock from Didlington Hall, Norfolk.

56

Photographs: John Baxter

furnishings with him. These were lost in a fire at Fort George; and his claim for loss gives an itemized list of furniture, paintings, library, porcelains, curtains, chandeliers, etc., which has served as an invaluable guide in acquiring the present furnishings. As the building was not only residence but seat of government, many of the family rooms were on the second story. The upstairs sitting room is quietly formal and is given dignity by its handsome English paneling from Teddesley Hall, Penkridge, Staffordshire. In its pedimented overmantel panel hangs a view of a late seventeenth-century English country seat of the type which colonial builders, particularly in the South, endeavored to reproduce on simplified scale. The room has an antique English needlework carpet in dark brown with flowers of faded crimson and soft blue shades that suggested the use of blue lampas covering for the Chippendale armchairs, and for the curtains. A note of intense blue is provided by the Bilston enamel cassolettes on the mantel shelf. The woodwork combines two shades of soft gray-blue; the walls are off-white.

57

THE LIVING ROOM

The dignity of an English paneled room with Grinling Gibbons carving of fruit and game around the fireplace is emphasized in Mr. and Mrs. Charles Blyth's Burlingame house by great furniture of the William Kent and Chippendale periods.

The superlatively fine bookcase and desk with veneered panels of richly figured walnut is in Kent's best architectural style, and the corner chair with unusually low and graceful back, used as a desk chair, is a handsome example of Queen Anne.

Eighteenth-century needlework on the Chippendale armchair by the door and other examples of petit point and crewelwork in rich colors are of museum quality.

Portraits by Lawrence and Romney and a rare pair of English luster chandeliers with delicate canopies and urn-shaped stems are among the Georgian masterpieces in this elegant room looking out onto a magnificently kept lawn and formal garden framed by the tall eucalyptuses of the California coast.

HOUSE IN BURLINGAME
California

HOME OF MR. AND MRS. CHARLES BLYTH

Photographs: Jerome Zerbe

Tulip hinge from cupboard opposite.

Rare inlaid dated chest, 1780.

LONGAGO

Brandywine Hundred, Delaware

HOME OF MR. AND MRS. TITUS C. GEESEY

THE DINING ROOM

In this Pennsylvania-German interior, the mellow brown tone of walnut and pine imparts its glow to a setting enlivened with red, green, and yellow in the painted decoration of furniture, pottery, and fractur. The last consists of the birth-and-baptismal certificates, house blessings, and other documents decorated with calligraphy, tulips, birds, and hearts, which represent a most individual folk art. All the pieces are the work of settlers from the Rhineland and other parts of Central Europe who came in the eighteenth century to Lancaster, Lebanon, Berks, and Montgomery counties of Pennsylvania.

The dresser and the cupboard with glazed doors both contain many signed and dated examples of sgraffito and slip-decorated pottery. The red body of the earthenware, which shows through the scratched decoration, and the cream color of the slip, with additional touches of dark green and red in the figure and flower designs, produce a subdued but rich color harmony. The cupboard has paneled doors below, with rattail hinges ending in a tulip, a favorite Pennsylvania-German motif, shown in detail on the opposite page. On top are a Schimmel eagle and rooster on either side of a woven straw and hickory basket for *schnitz* or dried apples.

The long wooden bowl on top of the dresser is for preparing stuffing for roast goose. In the center is a ten-foot stretcher table of walnut and pine from the old General Wayne Inn, covered with a red and white checked cloth on which are pottery plates, candlesticks, and a decorated milk pan signed by the elder Paul Bell, first of the Shenandoah Valley potters. A carved and inlaid "Kentucky" rifle, actually made in Pennsylvania but once thought to have been made in Kentucky because so many of them were found there, hangs over the fireplace.

VAN CORTLANDT HOUSE 1748

Van Cortlandt Park, New York

NATIONAL SOCIETY OF COLONIAL DAMES IN THE STATE OF NEW YORK

THE EAST PARLOR

Ever since 1897 the Van Cortlandt house has been open to the public. The Colonial Dames are custodians of the house, which was presented to the state in 1886 by descendants of the builder, Frederick Van Cortlandt, and his wife, Frances Jay, who lived here in something like baronial state on the banks of Mosholu Brook. This should not be confused with the manor house of Van Cortlandt shown on pages 144–145.

The East Parlor became the most important room in the house, superseding the West Parlor some years after its original building in 1748. Probably not long after the middle of the century, handsome alterations were made, especially to the paneling around the fireplace.

Long continued work to perfect the restoration of the interior has resulted in many changes and additions since 1897, as increasing knowledge of eighteenth-century precedent has been gained. However, some of the earlier acquisitions, made before

1920, are of the highest importance. One of these is the handsome New England secretary, which once belonged to the early collector, Richard Canfield. It used to be called a Newport piece but is now recognized as very probably the work of a Massachusetts cabinetmaker. Another early gift was the extremely fine large piecrust table, which came down in the Frelinghuysen family with the tradition that it had been presented by General Nathanael Greene of Rhode Island to an ancestor, Madame Van Vechten of Finderne, New Jersey, as a mark of appreciation for having been allowed to stay at her house during the winter of Valley Forge.

The needlework on the fire screen was done in red, blue, green, brown and beige tones by a lady of the Beekman family, whose portrait hangs at the left of the fireplace. The spinet was made in London in 1771. Curtains are of yellow damask and the cushions in the window recesses are covered in yellow silk. The walls and paneling of oyster white provide a traditional background for the portraits and mahogany furniture.

Photographs: Gottscho-Schleisner

THE SCHUYLER MANSION

Albany, New York

THE STATE OF NEW YORK

THE NORTHEAST PARLOR

While Philip Schuyler was in London in 1761-1762 his new house, called "The Pastures," was being built under a friend's supervision, and when he sailed up the

Hudson on his return it had practically been completed. In 1780 his daughter Elizabeth was married to Alexander Hamilton here.

The Northeast Parlor, across the hall from the Hamilton Room, is especially handsome. At the windows, hung with draperies of crimson worsted, are two remarkably fine New York armchairs that were owned by Philip Schuyler. The tea chest on the table between them is a Schuyler family piece. A portrait of Philip's daughter-in-law, Sarah Rutsen, wife of Philip Jeremiah Schuyler, hangs above the Chippendale sofa.

Photographs: Gottscho-Schleisner

The New England secretary and gilt Chippendale mirror came to the house after its acquisition by the state in 1911 as the gift of Georgiana and Louisa Lee Schuyler. Other presentations of family heirlooms have made it possible to furnish half of the lower floor with Schuyler pieces. A gift from J. P. Morgan is the chairback settee, unusual in American work but possibly of Philadelphia make. The New England chest-on-chest behind it was the gift of George D. Pratt.

The side chair at the tea table is especially appropriate here, for it is of a design based on Chippendale that was followed in America only by New York chairmakers.

MOUNT PLEASANT
Fairmount Park, Philadelphia
THE CITY OF PHILADELPHIA

THE UPSTAIRS PARLOR

Much is known of a long succession of owners of Mount Pleasant, but the name historians of architecture most desire, that of the architect and builder of this great country seat, is not recorded. An English origin could be suspected, as the plan of the house and dependencies, and the exterior and interior decoration, show a high degree of skill and training.

Photographs: the Philadelphia Museum of Art

Built in 1761 for Captain John Macpherson, who had made a fortune privateering in the West Indies, this house of stuccoed fieldstone on a bluff above the Schuyl-kill was doubtless furnished originally with the same kind of fine Philadelphia furniture that the Museum has sought for it today—the work of Affleck, Gostelowe, Randolph, and other cabinetmakers who made "Philadelphia Chippendale" the rich-est American style.

The parlor has superbly carved paneling above the fireplace, a paneled dado, and pedimented doors leading to the hall. A Philadelphia secretary with a scrolled top and an English mirror with a delicately poised phoenix as a finial are noteworthy for their rich carving. The side table, a Philadelphia rococo masterpiece, has an un-usual apron, or frieze, made graceful with C-scrolls on either side of a carved shell.

The walls and cornice of the room are painted in an ashes-of-roses shade, and the silk brocade curtains are of scarlet and gold.

67

Photographs: Gilbert Ask

MOUNT CUBA

Greenville, Delaware

HOME OF MR. AND MRS. LAMMOT DU PONT COPELAND

THE DINING ROOM

The dining room in this Georgian-style contemporary home is lined with eighteenth-century paneling from a house in Stafford County, Virginia. The walls have been painted yellow to harmonize with the antique gold damask curtains.

With the exception of the table, which is English, most of the furniture was made in Philadelphia; the highboy with pierced finial represents the finest Philadelphia work, and the butler's chest of drawers (shown in the photograph above) is outstanding for the fretwork carving on the chamfered corners. The slab-top Queen Anne table next to it is one of several of this rare type of eighteenth-century design in the house.

An English painting of game birds in a landscape hangs in its original frame over the fireplace; and to the left, through the doorway, we glimpse the Chinese painted paper shown in larger detail in the view of the hall on the opposite page. Imported as early as 1700 from England, papers like these were known in fine homes in the colonies from early times. As they were mounted on cloth, the old records referred to them as "hangings." This treatment has undoubtedly insured their survival; they serve as the perfect setting for Chippendale furniture.

SOTTERLEY
Hollywood, St. Marys County, Maryland

SOTTERLEY MANSION FOUNDATION

THE DRAWING ROOM

Sotterley, architecturally informal in its exterior, is famous for its eighteenth-century woodwork, especially the graceful shell alcoves in the drawing room and a Chinese Chippendale lattice stairway in the hall. Rich interiors were added by the Plater family

70

in mid-eighteenth century to a house begun before 1730. In that year they acquired the estate, known as Bowles Preservation, part of a grant from Lord Baltimore in 1650. They renamed it Sotterley after the family home in Suffolk, England.

Because the English Sotterley was also associated with the Satterlee family, the house attracted the interest of Herbert L. Satterlee of New York, who purchased it in 1910. He furnished it with a collection of rare English and American antiques to which his daughter, Mrs. Mabel Satterlee Ingalls, who inherited Sotterley in 1947, has added. The intimate character of a house furnished to be lived in has not been lost since it was opened to the public in 1953. It is now under the direction of a foundation created in 1962.

Photographs: Louis H. Frohman

Photographs: Jerome Zerbe

HOUSE-ON-HILL
San Mateo, California
HOME OF MRS. TOBIN CLARK

THE LIBRARY

While the lover of books resents the suggestion that they be used as decoration, his heart warms to the sight of red and green morocco bindings in tall shelves reaching to the ceiling of a paneled room.

In the arrangement of this beautiful library in Mrs. Tobin Clark's house near San Francisco (designed by David Adler), much thought has been given to the creation of surroundings that answer the needs of solitude, writing, quiet reading—and good conversation as well.

The background is subdued through the absence of all patterned fabrics, and this contributes to the pleasant atmosphere of restfulness. The only exception to the ban on pattern is the firescreen, with its early eighteenth-century English needlework in reds, blues, brown, and beige tones.

The antique pine paneling has its climax in the long swags of fruit hanging from bowknots at the fireplace, carved in high relief and with the vibrant form that marks the style of Grinling Gibbons.

An early eighteenth-century brass chandelier, recalling the Dutch seventeenth-century chandeliers seen in paintings by Terborch, is perfect here, where the mid-Georgian chandelier of glass would be making too early an appearance. On the other hand, the Chippendale library table, also mid-Georgian, is not out of place. This offers a good example of the rule that walls and lighting devices should represent the same period, while furniture of many periods can be mixed successfully. Reynolds' portrait of Doctor Samuel Johnson is unusual in that it shows the famous lexicographer without a wig.

THE PARLOR

There are, at Shelburne, many reminders of early rural life and the homespun crafts that have long interested the founder of its museum, Mrs. J. Watson Webb. There are also collections of another sort, well represented in this room. Here New England furniture can be studied in examples as fine as may be seen in any museum in America.

THE VERMONT HOUSE

Shelburne Museum, Shelburne, Vermont

Photographs: Taylor & Dull

The Newport armchair at the right of the fireplace, with arms terminating in carved parrot heads, is literally unique. The octagonal tea table at the left of the fireplace is also a Newport piece and is the only known example in the eight-sided form from this Rhode Island town. The Queen Anne secretary (opposite) is believed to be the work of Benjamin Burnham, Colchester, Connecticut, who signed a desk now in the Metropolitan Museum. Also in the parlor is a Connecticut cherry lowboy with leaf, shell, and heart carving. These motifs are all suggestive of Connecticut but used in an entirely individual manner.

The Vermont House, a stone house built shortly after 1790, was brought from the eastern part of Shelburne Township when it was in danger of destruction in 1947. The paneling in the parlor, from a house in Essex, Connecticut, has an early type of arched paneling, painted a bluish green. The plaster walls are oyster white. The draperies have a floral design in wool in shades of blue, tan, brown, and rose on a cream ground.

WINTERTHUR
Delaware

THE HENRY FRANCIS DU PONT WINTERTHUR MUSEUM

THE PINE KITCHEN

The timeless charm of country furniture is very well represented by this eighteenth-century pine-paneled kitchen which was once installed at Winterthur. The green Windsors around the Pennsylvania sawbuck table have their old coloring, green being a popular color for these chairs originally. There is a fine group of Windsor types here: hoop-back, comb-back, and lowback, and a choice settee with carved knuckle arms at the left of the fireplace. The table is set with wooden trenchers, pewter pitcher, and covered dish, and eighteenth-century tumblers and wine bottles of dark green blown glass. A tin chandelier, crudely formed and very decorative, is an attractive early lighting device. At the right of the fireplace is a high-backed settee which is more elaborate than usual, having a paneled back instead of a plain one. The spoonrack in the corner is filled with pewter spoons, and there are many examples of American pewter, including marked pieces, displayed on the dressers in this room along with Pennsylvania sgraffito pottery and New England slipware. The great fireplace is equipped for cooking with wrought-iron cranes, trammels, spits, and trivets; and there are iron, brass, and copper pots, kettles, ladles, and skimmers. A rifle and powder horn hang above the fireplace.

A very rare example of an eighteenth-century floor covering has been placed under the table. This covering, which was known as a floorcloth, was made of thick canvas heavily coated with layers of paint, the top layer being painted in a design either like inlaid marble (such as the lozenge pattern here) or taken from contemporary woven carpets. Because of hard wear, generally only fragments survive; this complete example is the finest known.

THE HAMPTON ROOM

Newport and Massachusetts furniture in this room include a Chippendale bed with reeded posts and cabriole legs that is considered the finest example of its period in the Winterthur collection. The Newport block-front secretary with its carved shells and reeded urn finials represents the Townsend-Goddard family of cabinetmakers, whose work is also seen in the block-front chest of drawers at the opposite wall.

The bed hangings, window draperies, and upholstery of the easy chair and slipper chair are in printed English linen. The paneling, from a house built in 1761 in

Photograph: Ivan Dmitri

77

Photographs: Gottscho-Schleisner; courtesy Winterthur Museum

WINTERTHUR (*Continued*)

Elizabeth, New Jersey, is in an urbane style that allies it closely with Philadelphia work, particularly Woodford in Fairmount Park, built in 1756.

The carved tabernacle overmantel frames a New Jersey landscape showing a view across the Delaware to the present League Island. It was painted for Fancy Hill, the home of Samuel Ladd Howell at Gloucester, New Jersey. A collection of Worcester porcelain transfer-printed in black is displayed in the cupboard, and a Holland Delft garniture stands on the mantel. The carpet of geometric design is an Ushak of a type used in colonial America.

THE MAPLE ROOM

The paneling in this room at Winterthur comes from Port Royal, a home built in 1762 by a wealthy West Indian planter at Frankford, north of Philadelphia. It has its original paint surface, the mellowed hues of which are in perfect harmony with the honey-colored tone of the Chippendale maple furniture, the homespun glazed wool hangings of the bed, and the quilted bedspread. The black seen in the ground of the rare eighteenth-century English Wilton carpet is introduced again with striking emphasis in the English Jackfield tea-and-coffee set just visible in the corner of the photograph.

The painting is a conversation piece, a type rare in America but frequently seen in England. It is the work of William Williams, a decorative painter who first instructed the young Benjamin West and worked in the middle colonies for thirty years before returning to England.

Photograph: Gottscho-Schleisner; courtesy Winterthur Museum

WINTERTHUR (*Continued*)

THE BERTRAND PARLOR

80

The paneling of the walls of this room as far only as a high dado represents a change in style from the earlier fully paneled room. The new style came into use about the middle of the eighteenth century. The paneling is a particularly suitable background for the Chippendale furniture, made after 1760.

Most of these pieces, collected by Mr. du Pont, were made in New York. They include a typical serpentine gaming table with heavily gadrooned apron, four ruffle-and-tassel-back side chairs, and a pair of chairs (against the wall) with pierced diamond splat resembling the work of Gilbert Ash, whose hand is possibly to be seen in the tripod tea table between them.

Brilliant color is given to the room by the red moreen upholstery and the crimson silk window hangings. The fabric in the hangings may be dated as early as 1725; and the Turkish carpet, which repeats their tones in a softened scale, is of the same period.

This parlor is a Virginia room, brought to Winterthur from Belle Isle, the home built by William Bertrand in Lancaster County before 1760. The painted mantel, from a late eighteenth-century Virginia house, has English delft tiles around the opening of the fireplace.

GUNSTON HALL 1755
Lorton, Virginia
THE NATIONAL SOCIETY OF
COLONIAL DAMES OF AMERICA

THE PALLADIAN ROOM

Photograph: James R. Dunlop

The drawing room at Gunston Hall is one of the finest Palladian interiors in America. Gunston was built by the statesman George Mason, author of the Virginia Declaration of Rights. Young William Buckland, fresh from England in 1755, was resident architect and carver. The Gunston interiors represent his earliest work in America; his later style is represented at Annapolis.

Photograph: James R. Dunlop

Photograph: Charles Baptie

The window enframement shows familiarity with English works in architecture, of which Buckland is known to have had seventeen volumes, while most colonial builders had only three or four. The door illustrated is one of five original paneled doors. As to the walls, old tack marks were discovered which indicated an original covering of fabric; and red damask, known to have been an eighteenth-century favorite, was used here in the restoration. The fireplace wall is putty color. An English glass chandelier with faceted arms is of a type that could have been imported prior to the Revolution.

The Philadelphia tripod tea table and side chairs, New York card table, and New England Queen Anne shell-crested side chair (at the window) are among the furnishings recently brought together for this room by the National Society of Colonial Dames, which has been working actively on the restoration of the house since 1949. The gardens have the finest box to be seen in Virginia.

Photograph: Charles Baptie

Photograph: Samuel Chamberlain

THE ALLEN HOUSE
Deerfield, Massachusetts

HOME OF MR. AND MRS. HENRY N. FLYNT

Photograph: Taylor & Dull

84

THE NORTH CHAMBER

In this house, their own residence, as well as in the historic house museums which they have furnished at Deerfield, Mr. and Mrs. Flynt have brought together many pieces of seventeenth- and eighteenth-century furniture made in the Connecticut Valley, where Deerfield is situated. The secretary is such a piece, possibly made by the Chapins of East Windsor and Hartford, since the finial is of the pierced type found on their highboys.

Textiles and embroideries are notable at Deerfield, and include such unusual examples as the blue and white bed hangings shown in detail opposite. These are copper-plate printed with a pastoral design of French character; but the fabric is actually of English origin, bearing the stamp of the maker, *R. Jones 1761.*

The Allen House, one of the historic homes of Deerfield, was occupied by the schoolteacher Hannah Beaman, who held her school here after she returned from captivity among the Indians following the Deerfield Massacre of 1704.

85

THE WEBB HOUSE 1752
Wethersfield, Connecticut
NATIONAL SOCIETY OF COLONIAL DAMES OF
AMERICA IN THE STATE OF CONNECTICUT

THE COUNCIL ROOM

The Council Room of the Webb House is so-called because it became the conference room of Washington and Rochambeau in May, 1781, when the former, accompanied by General Knox, journeyed from the Hudson to confer with Rochambeau and Chastellux, who had come from Newport. The plan of campaign worked out here resulted in the victory at Yorktown the following October.

86

Photographs: Alexander Bender

The paneling, an important example of mid-eighteenth-century Connecticut architecture, is found throughout the house. Walls and woodwork are off-white. Particularly unusual is the position of the summer beam parallel to the fireplace instead of at right angles to it, a deviation from the usual form of construction.

The house was built by Joseph Webb in 1752 and incorporates an ell of seventeenth-century date. Since its acquisition by the Colonial Dames, the house has been furnished with appropriate examples of eighteenth-century furniture, including Webb family pieces. There are fine examples of porcelain and glass, the library is rich in eighteenth-century titles, and some especially fine embroideries and textiles are to be found in other rooms.

The wallpaper in the Council Room is a reproduction of an early design. Green predominates, with gold and black on a white ground.

TOURELLE

Southampton, New York

A FRENCH ROOM IN A LONG ISLAND HOME

THE SITTING ROOM

A French room with *boiserie* of the Louis XV period and furniture by the *maîtres ébénistes* of Paris shows the subtly curving forms that are so distinctively and agreeably French.

The French *ébéniste,* carver, and metalworker thought of use and function as well as beauty. They managed to prove that the practical and the frivolous, the functional and the ornate, were compatible.

The age which said that "style is the man" gave attention to style in all things—in deportment, in writing a letter, in decorating a porcelain garniture, or in designing the ormolu mounts on furniture.

To bring together the arts of this exacting period in a modern room without turning it into a museum is not easy. That it can be done, however, without loss of intimate charm is admirably demonstrated in this Long Island home.

88

THE BOUCHER ROOM

It is fitting that the home and art collections of Henry Clay Frick, 1849-1919, should be represented by the arts of France, for this was his first interest.

The sight of the French art in the Wallace Collection in London first gave Mr. Frick a definite impulse to create something similar for America. The Boucher Room, which he acquired in 1916 for the mansion that Carrère & Hastings had designed for him and which faces Central Park on Fifth Avenue, had recently passed through the Wertheimer and Maurice Kann collections but came originally from the Château de Crécy near Dreux. These decorations were painted by Boucher for Madame de Pompadour during remodeling of the château, which she acquired in 1746. She spent far more than the purchase price of 650,000 livres in making it resplendent, and it was ready for the reception of the king in 1755.

The paintings, which were executed between 1751 and 1755, are related to Boucher's panels in the Salle du Conseil at Fontainebleau (1752-1753). The subjects are personifications of the arts, sciences, and occupations of men represented by delightful children. The eight panels, originally designed for an octagonal room, show Architecture and Chemistry, Comedy and Tragedy, Singing and Dancing, Painting and Sculpture, Fowling and Horticulture, Poetry and Music, Astronomy and

THE FRICK MANSION
New York City

A ROOM CREATED FOR MADAME DE POMPADOUR

Hydraulics, Fishing and Hunting. The rosy-cheeked pairs of children in sunny landscapes under cerulean and azure skies seem like flowers themselves, with their pink fingers and bare feet, surrounded by festoons of anemones, roses, larkspur, ranunculus, and pimpernel. The blue of the sky colors is repeated in the fabrics that cover the Louis XV chairs. A fine Louis XVI *bureau plat* of *acajou* (mahogany) with gilt-bronze mounts stands near the Louis XV marble mantel which has a porcelain garniture from Sèvres, a factory which owed much to the support of Mme. de Pompadour.

Photographs: Harold Haliday Costain

BONNIE DOON

Ritter, South Carolina

HOME OF ALFRED H. CASPARY

THE LIVING ROOM

The combination of English Queen Anne and Chippendale furniture, sporting paintings, and fine Oriental porcelains was so brilliantly exemplified at the home of the famous philatelist and art collector, the late Alfred H. Caspary, that this final impression of his winter home has a lasting interest for those who live with antiques.

The Caspary porcelains are now in the Philadelphia Museum of Art, paintings by Ferneley have gone back to England, the fine English furniture has passed through the auction room.

This important and historic room has been included for its documentary value. It records some of the discriminating standards of our own day in decorating with eighteenth-century antiques.

THE JEREMIAH LEE MANSION 1768

Marblehead, Massachusetts

THE MARBLEHEAD HISTORICAL SOCIETY

THE STATE CHAMBER

Lee Mansion is now the only house in this country where old English *painted* scenic wallpaper is still in place. The other famous example, the Van Rensselaer wallpaper, was taken to the Metropolitan Museum some years ago.

Photographs: Samuel Chamberlain

94

Colonel Jeremiah Lee spent over ten thousand pounds on his house and imported many of his furnishings from England. Its exceptional carved panels, cornices, and door frames alone would make the house distinguished. The painted papers showing Roman ruins are based on the work of Pannini and Vernet, and, with their broad ornamental borders, represent the height of rococo decoration. These painted papers (executed in tones of *grisaille*), are to be distinguished from the later block-printed scenic papers and are so rare that few are known even in England.

The original furnishings of the house have been long dispersed. For over a century the house served as a bank, but during this time the building, fortunately, was not changed structurally, and the papers here and in other parts of the house are remarkably well preserved.

Examples of New England William and Mary, Queen Anne, Chippendale, and Hepplewhite furniture decorate what has now become the headquarters of the Marblehead Historical Society. The Hepplewhite side chair at left of window is one from a set of six here which belonged to John Hancock.

95

Photographs: Karl Obert

THE SCULPTURE ROOM

An absorbing interest in Oriental art has led Avery Brundage to form one of the great private collections in America, many examples of which are now at La Pineta. European art is also an interest of Mr. and Mrs. Brundage, who have personally sought out on their European travels the fine pieces of Spanish, French, and Italian furniture and sculpture now at La Pineta, as well as in their Chicago home.

The beautiful fifteenth-century Florentine Madonna by Ghiberti stands between Spanish carved wood columns of the seventeenth century which were found in Spain several years ago, along with the little altar vases that accompany her in the detail photograph illustrated below.

The architecture of this large room which looks out into a formal garden and beyond to the distant Santa Ynéz Mountains, shows Spanish influence in the great beams of the ceiling and in the hooded fireplace. The furnishings, too, are predominantly Spanish. Chinese sculpture of the T'ang and Sung periods is richly represented; there is also the figure of Kwannon (shown in detail at right) which is considered unquestionably one of the finest medieval sculptures outside Japan.

Japanese gilt-wood sculpture of **Kwannon, Goddess of Mercy.**

Madonna by Ghiberti. 15th century.

Photographs: André Kertész

A HOUSE IN THE CITY

New York City

FORMERLY THE HOME OF MYRON C. TAYLOR

THE SALON

It requires perfect taste to bring together works of art of so many periods and countries. Here are elements from the fifteenth century to the eighteenth, with Impressionist paintings in addition. A sixteenth-century Spanish coffered ceiling that Mr. Taylor found in Spain determined the form of the room, which was literally built for it, its long narrow proportions giving full opportunity to appreciate the design of the carved brackets and the subdued brilliance of the old polychrome coloring. As in the Spanish palace from which it undoubtedly came, the walls of plaster are painted an oyster white. A fifteenth-century French stone mantel has a deeply carved floral frieze supported on slender colonnettes. A portrait of a youth by the Florentine painter, Bronzino, hangs above it.

Furniture consists chiefly of eighteenth-century French and Italian pieces, their lighter forms and embroidered upholstery coverings creating a much more inviting and livable effect than the Renaissance furniture which a collector not so many years ago would have undoubtedly placed in this setting.

One of Turner's golden Venetian scenes hangs over an Italian sofa in the Louis XVI style. In the hall, a fourteenth-century French sculpture of St. Catherine, in the dress of a noble lady of the court of Charles V, stands in half shadow. The architecture has been harmonized with the many Gothic works in the house by the use of pointed arches, in one of which hangs a fourteenth-century Italian primitive.

FILOLI

San Mateo, California

HOME OF MRS. WILLIAM P. ROTH

Above: La Promenade
Publique *by Debu-
court.*

Countess of Derby.
*Engraving by Barto-
lozzi.*

THE DRAWING ROOM

The superb proportions of this room, and sense of space, enhance the beauty of
the individual pieces contained in it. The keynote is struck by the great mantel,
dominant by its large scale but emphasizing delicacy of ornamentation. This is
repeated in the refinement of the pierced galleries of Chippendale tea tables and
the lightness of *chinoiserie* ornament on the Louis XV black and gold lacquer commode. The Ispahan floral rug is of the sixteenth-century and must, in its early
existence, have graced a palace.

This drawing room is also a gallery, in a sense, for it contains an exceptional collection of eighteenth-century English and French color prints. Bartolozzi's engraving of Lawrence's portrait of the actress Miss Farren, who became Countess of Derby, hangs by the door at the right. The other subject reproduced in detail on the opposite page, *La Promenade Publique,* a famous French print by Debucourt, shows a fashionable assemblage near the Circus of the Palais Royal. This print hangs to the right of the fireplace.

Photograph: Moulin Studios

Photographs: John Engstead

FRENCH HOUSE IN CALIFORNIA
Huntington Palisades, Los Angeles
HOME OF WILLIAM C. KENNEDY

THE SALON

A wrought-iron gateway, gabled front, and formal planting of box and Greek myrtle form an introduction to a superb collection of French eighteenth-century arts—furniture signed by famous *ébénistes*, sculpture, ceramics, paintings, and prints. A blue salon is the setting for a collection of blue and white faïence, chiefly Nevers and Rouen. Deep blue and ecru Utrecht velvet covers a pair of Louis XV winged *bérgères* which have the inventory mark of the Tuileries and are in their first paint. All other seat furniture in the house is signed. In this room are three chairs by Louis Cresson. They are accompanied by a *bureau plat* of tulipwood and amaranth with ormolu mounts, dated 1743, which are probably by Charles Cressent. The *chinoiserie* wall panel is by Pillement. A Louis XV rock-crystal chandelier complements this harmonious interior. In the dining room there is a collection of soft paste porcelain. Fruit,

102

flower, and vegetable designs are in evidence in these examples from Marseilles, Strasbourg, Münden, Kiel, Stralsund, and Brussels, and there is a very rare piece of Arnheim. Apricot-colored fabrics and celadon green walls take their cue from what could be called a garden in porcelain.

BOXWOOD

Atlanta, Georgia

HOME OF JAMES SWAN FLOYD

Photographs: Harold Haliday Costain

THE DRAWING ROOM

There is something about the view of the terrace at Boxwood, with its framework of iron lace, which immediately suggests America to the exclusion of all other places in the world. This house really could not be anywhere else.

Distinctively American, too, is the treatment of the drawing room with its fine antiques, many of which Mr. and Mrs. Floyd personally collected in Europe. The satinwood breakfront is filled with eighteenth-century porcelains, while other examples are used throughout the room to provide rich notes of color or effective contrasts of white, as supplied, for instance, by the Meissen birdcage.

The side chairs came from Haddon Hall and are, of course, Chippendale. Draperies with festooned valances of the Adam style are in keeping with the Adam mantel and the Adam commode (one of a pair) with painted designs in the style of Angelica Kaufmann.

The grillwork used in the architecture came from an old New Orleans house built in 1858.

104

KENMORE

Fredericksburg, Virginia

HOME OF FIELDING LEWIS AND BETTY WASHINGTON LEWIS, 1752

THE KENMORE ASSOCIATION

THE GREAT ROOM

It is evident from the stucco-duro decoration throughout Kenmore that Colonel Fielding Lewis spared little expense in preparing a handsome and formal house for his bride, the sister of George Washington. Some students believe that embellishment of stone or stucco was intended for the quite plain exterior of Kenmore, but that work was halted by the Revolution, during which Fielding Lewis ruined himself financially by outfitting three regiments at his own expense.

Photographs: Arnold Newman

The stucco work was done probably by a French workman who also decorated ceilings at Mount Vernon. His most elaborate handiwork is seen at Kenmore, appearing in all the rooms on the ground floor save the office.

The design of the bas relief over the fireplace illustrates Aesop's fable of "The Fox, the Crow, and the Piece of Cheese," and is said to have been suggested by Washington as a lesson for the children, warning them of the danger of flattery. The armchairs at the fireplace were owned by Charles Washington. The chandelier, an exceptionally fine one, was made about 1760 in England.

The carving on the mantel frieze, the rectangular frame of the overmantel, the handsome cornice, and the rich plasterwork on the ceiling make this room one of the handsomest eighteenth-century interiors in America.

THE NORTHEAST PARLOR

During the Revolution this house was the headquarters of the French Admiral de Ternay. Its last owner, a Loyalist, Joseph Wanton, Jr., had fled, and the house was confiscated. It was one of the most luxurious mansions in Newport, and the superlative quality of its architectural detail is evident in the number of bolection moldings on the paneled walls.

In this parlor the carved Corinthian pilasters, marbleized in black and gold (the original treatment) are possibly unique. The walls have been repainted a putty shade, which is the color they originally were.

THE HUNTER HOUSE
Newport, Rhode Island
PRESERVATION SOCIETY OF NEWPORT COUNTY

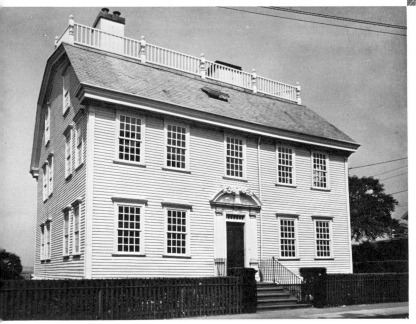

The Preservation Society, which acquired the house in 1945 and restored it, intends to make it a museum of the arts and crafts of Newport and is acquiring a permanent collection of the work of the Goddards, Townsends, and other Newport craftsmen, many of whom worked within a few hundred yards of this house.

THE CORBIT-SHARP HOUSE

Odessa, Delaware

THE WINTERTHUR CORPORATION

THE DRAWING ROOM

The drawing room in the Corbit House, with its chimney breast crowned by a broken-pitch pediment and flanked by fluted pilasters, may have been suggested by the published works of the English architect Abraham Swan. Obviously this room is closely related to the one from the Powel House now in the Philadelphia Museum of Art.

Whether the carpenter, Robert May, whose bills for the Corbit House still exist, came from Philadelphia is not known, but his work is seen in other houses in Odessa. The house shows many rich details for the home of a young Quaker, William Corbit. His familiarity with city styles resulted from two years' apprenticeship in Philadelphia, where he learned the tanning trade in order to establish what became a highly profitable business at the market town of Odessa, then called Cantwell's Bridge. His desire to build the finest mansion in the Delaware Valley was realized in this Georgian house, built in 1772, with a Chinese fret railing on the hip roof, granite lintels over the windows, and an imposing doorway. The house was acquired in 1938 by H. Rodney Sharp, who restored it and made it his home until 1958, when he presented it to the Winterthur Corporation.

At the drawing room fireplace a New York Chippendale easy chair of about 1760 confronts a slightly earlier Philadelphia Queen Anne easy chair with trifid foot. Other fine examples of Queen Anne and Chippendale furniture, chiefly from the middle colonies, live up to the dignity of this rich architectural setting. The family group in a landscape over the mantel is attributed to William Williams (active 1746-1766).

The woodwork in this room is a gray-blue, popular in the eighteenth century, and the plaster walls are a light salmon pink.

DRAYTON

Towson

A HOME IN MARYLAND

THE LIVING ROOM

The medallion relief on the early nineteenth-century mantel of this room shows *The Battle of Lake Erie*. The design is based on an engraving issued soon after the event. Above it on the frieze is an inscription giving Perry's famous message, *We have met the enemy and they are ours*. Obviously this is a rare memento of the enthusiasm over the American naval victory of September 10, 1813. Perry's portrait is shown on the left, facing Franklin, who was probably chosen because this mantel was made in Pennsylvania.

Some especially distinguished pieces of American furniture are to be seen in the room. The Philadelphia highboy is of the highest quality and of early date, probably about 1750, indicated by use of the trifid foot rather than claw and ball. The small Hepplewhite mirror is a rare example made in America, and the Sheraton Martha Washington chair one of the finest of its kind. A rare sequence of tables consists of a Queen Anne tilt-top, a Philadelphia piecrust with handsomely carved tripod, and a Duncan Phyfe library table. The glass chandelier is English, its notched arms indicating a date about 1775.

Photographs: Harold Haliday Costain

WIDEHALL

Chestertown, Kent County, Maryland

HOME OF MRS. WILBUR W. HUBBARD

THE PARLOR

The handsome little town house with its Georgian architecture and ivy-clad walls was built at the time of Chestertown's greatness as a port of entry.

The name "Widehall" appears self-explained by the unusual and very striking design of the hall. This is crossed by three large, keystoned arches shown in the detailed architectural view above. Through the doorway from the hall is a view of the parlor with an extremely beautiful paneled fireplace. This displays the familiarity of the builder with English architectural works.

The house is mid-eighteenth century and was built for an unknown owner, though he was doubtless one of the many merchants of the Eastern Shore who found trade profitable with the West Indies.

The rooms in Mrs. Hubbard's home are formal yet delightfully livable. Interiors appear even more spacious in their light colors and the furniture is both tastefully selected and arranged in keeping with the period and everyday needs of comfort and hospitable entertaining. It is the sum total, the atmosphere, of Widehall that makes it so pleasantly gracious.

HOUSE IN BRYN MAWR
Pennsylvania

HOME OF MRS. J. STOGDELL STOKES

THE LIVING ROOM

Mr. J. Stogdell Stokes, for many years president of the Philadelphia Museum of Art, was a devoted student of the crafts of Pennsylvania, particularly of Chester County, and also of neighboring New Jersey and the Pennsylvania-German region. For many years Mr. and Mrs. Stokes added to their collections, and after his death in 1947 many pieces passed to the Museum.

A few years ago Mrs. Stokes selected her favorite objects and built a new home for them, designed by the architect Sydney E. Martin. The house has an eighteenth-century air, and is typical of Chester County.

The slipware plates on the mantel are from a large collection of Pennsylvania pottery. At either end of the mantel is an unusual three-branched iron candelabrum, one of many early lighting devices seen throughout the house.

Photographs: Cortlandt V. D. Hubbard

In the view of a corner of the living room (top of opposite page), a fine Philadelphia Queen Anne side chair stands by a Queen Anne walnut dressing table or lowboy with graceful arched skirt. The fretwork mirror above has the label of Philadelphia's best-known maker of looking glasses, John Elliott. To the left, in the hall, is a tall clock signed by the early Philadelphia clockmaker, Peter Stretch (1670-1746). On the trestle table behind the sofa shown above (and again in the view opposite which was taken from dining room) note the fine Schimmel eagle with outspread wings.

117

BEAUPORT

Gloucester, Massachusetts

SOCIETY FOR THE PRESERVATION OF NEW ENGLAND ANTIQUITIES

Photographs: Samuel Chamberlain

THE CHINESE ROOM

The fresh coloring of this eighteenth-century Chinese wallpaper, dominated by cobalt blue and malachite green, is due to the fact that it had remained untouched in a Marblehead attic for one hundred and fifty years and was never on the wall until it was brought to Beauport. The design represents the industries of China, particularly tea culture and porcelain making. The scenes show picturesque views of houses, buildings, shops, and figures, colorfully depicted with touches of vermilion, red, rose-pink and sand color intermingled among the dominant tones of blue. The paper is similar to that in a room at Winterthur and it has been suggested that it is part of the same set, imported for "Morris's Folly," a town house that was begun in 1793 for Robert Morris, financier of the Revolution, but never finished because of his financial failure in the China trade. The papers were apparently disposed of by the sea captain or merchant who brought them from the Orient. They are remarkable for their pictorial designs in contrast to the usual flower and bird patterns on many Chinese papers.

A magnificent English cut-glass chandelier of about 1765 lights the room, which is furnished with English Chippendale pieces, many of them in the Chinese taste, and a few in the Gothic style. It is the most consistent in adherence to a single style of any room at Beauport, a house where its creator, Henry Davis Sleeper, delighted to bring together a profusion of styles and periods. In 1942 it was presented to the Society as a memorial to Helena Woolworth McCann by members of her family.

Photographs: *Jerome Zerbe*

THE SALON

This beautiful Florida house, which has recently become the home of another great collector of French art, Mme. Jacques Balsan, is seen here as it appeared when Mrs. Emory brought some of her fine French furniture and porcelains to her winter home at fashionable Palm Beach.

The great mirrored wall between the columns would have greatly pleased the French eighteenth-century decorators, particularly de Cotte, architect of Louis XV, who seems to have been the first to use mirrors in place of paintings, and to introduce them everywhere in the room. The size of the mirror panels with which the modern decorator can work would have drawn his envy, for he had to build up large areas through the use of narrow moldings. The mirror wall here supports a magnificent cartel clock, set in a sunburst of gilt rays.

A pair of armoires, their solid paneled doors replaced by glass, displays part of a notable collection of French and Meissen porcelain.

DUCK CREEK
Old Lyme, Connecticut
HOME OF J. A. LLOYD HYDE

THE SALON

In describing this remarkable house which was built and furnished in the 1940's by the late Arvid O. Knudson, Mr. Hyde calls it "a potpourri of antique French paneling and parquet floors, Italian marble, Chinese and French wallpapers, Thai and Chinese silks, Chinese and French porcelains, and French and English furniture." The result is one of the most fascinating homes in America.

Faïence cupids: c.1780

Photograph: Taylor & Dull; courtesy of Antiques

The Louis XVI mirror in the salon is believed to have come from the Palace of Versailles, and the parquet floor was found at Fontainebleau. The Aubusson tapestry portrays Louis XV at the chase. Louis XVI chairs and the sofa at the fireplace are white, a style favored in the eighteenth century in Sweden, where French furniture was in great demand. The use of blue and white checked linen to cover the backs of the chairs is in the eighteenth-century French style.

123

THE DINING ROOM

This room is in the same house as the salon reproduced on the preceding two pages.

The antique green satin curtains, which strike the note of color echoed in the tone of the oval backs of the Louis XVI chairs, once belonged to the Misses Hewitt, well remembered as generous patrons of the Cooper Union Museum.

Over a red marble mantel hangs a mirror that originally belonged to the Duchesse d'Angoulème, daughter of Louis XVI. The shelves, reaching all the way to the cornice over a Louis XVI commode, are arranged with a dinner service of Creil earthenware, transfer-printed in black, in a manner which makes them a particularly effective part of the decoration of the room.

The pagoda centerpiece of Sheffield plate from an inn at Brighton, England, and white Carrara marble floor from a house on Fifth Avenue, New York, are among the many elements that the creator of this matchless house, Arvid O. Knudson, gathered together from Europe, New England, and the Far East and united under one roof with imagination, taste, and style.

Sheffield plate pagoda: c.1800

HOUSE IN GREENWICH

Connecticut

HOME OF MR. AND MRS. FREDERIC C. PECK

THE LIVING ROOM

French furniture of the simpler type that can be found in Parisian work as well as in Provincial is grouped around the fireplace in this Connecticut living room.

The room is dominated by an unusually handsome Louis XV *trumeau,* or mirror with painted panel. The architectural frame has rococo ornament in gray which,

Photographs: Taylor & Dull

with the red and green of the decorative painting of birds, has set the color scheme for the rest of the room. The colors are repeated in the gray-green draperies and carpet, and an Aubusson rug in soft shades of red, ranging from dark rose to copper. The Louis XVI *bergères* that stand on it are covered in rust-colored velvet.

On the other side of the room are Louis XV fruitwood armchairs upholstered in rose-red leather (see top of opposite page). The coffee table between them is made of an old red tôle plate-warmer with *chinoiserie* decoration in gold. On either side of the mahogany chairback settee are small tables supporting lamps with bases made of tall, icicle-shaped French glass paperweights which are collectors' items.

127

Photographs: Harold Haliday Costain

THE DRAWING ROOM

A drawing room in Georgian style with fine English Chippendale carved mahogany furniture, Chinese painted panels and porcelain, and colorful needlework upholstery has all the elements of sophistication so well understood in the eighteenth century.

On the pedimented chimney-breast is an overmantel painting showing Italy's classic ruins that inspired English architects from Inigo Jones to Robert Adam in the shaping of the fashions represented here.

A terminus to successive adaptations of classic designs came during the Regency in the early nineteenth century. This period is represented in the hall, where the furniture offers an effective contrast, through restraint of line, to the more opulent forms of Chippendale in the drawing room.

Combined with formality and good taste are the warm personal touches that make this Atlanta home so invitingly contemporary and livable.

128

MIMOSA HALL

Rosswell, Cobb County, Georgia

HOME OF MR. AND MRS. GRANGER HANSELL

Photographs: Harold Haliday Costain

THE DRAWING ROOM

Twin fireplaces give distinctive character to this drawing room in Cobb County, Georgia. The matching convex mirrors hanging above them emphasize the unusual dual feature.

The arrangement we see is a modern one, although in an old home that has been in the possession of the owners' family for several generations.

The elegant furnishings combine French eighteenth-century pieces and English Hepplewhite, with a Regency oval table on dolphin supports and a charming pair of small Empire love seats.

The original house was burned shortly after it was completed in 1830. It was rebuilt in 1840 in its present form of brick and stucco, fronted by the classic white columns of the Greek Revival style that was interpreted so handsomely in Georgia.

Photographs: Samuel Chamberlain

THE PINGREE HOUSE
Salem, Massachusetts
THE ESSEX INSTITUTE

THE CROWNINSHIELD BEDROOM

The Adam style, which Samuel McIntire adapted to the needs of Salem ship owners who were building homes after the end of the eighteenth century, has an especially important example here. This house, built for John Gardner in 1804, has, through

later ownership, become known as the Pingree House. The heirs of David Pingree deeded it to the Essex Institute in 1933, and today it is one of the historic attractions of Salem.

The double parlor is justly famous and frequently illustrated, but other rooms, such as this bedroom, have as great a charm. It has been furnished chiefly with Salem pieces, including a marriage bed decorated with the quiver and torch of Eros, and hung with apricot taffeta and striped satin draperies. It was made about 1809 and has descended in a Salem family. A sofa of Grecian type is of slightly later date, about 1815-1820.

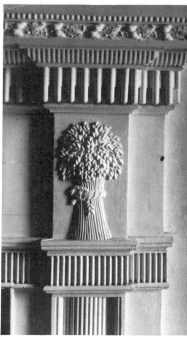

Over the mantel is a view of Salem harbor and the Crowninshield Wharf during the launching of the ship *Fame,* painted by George Ropes.

The glory of a McIntire house is in its ornamental detail, sometimes in composition, sometimes carved in wood. In the Pingree house the fine detail is carved, its perfection seen here in his favorite sheaf of wheat, a band of oak leaf, and a Pomona with a Horn of Plenty, all from the frieze on the mantel.

133

HOUSE. AT OYSTER BAY
Long Island, New York
HOME OF MR. AND MRS. REGINALD P. ROSE

Photographs: Taylor & Dull

THE DINING ROOM

The grace of the American Federal style in furniture is emphasized by the lofty curve of the unusual barrel-vaulted ceiling in this dining room, where festooned valances hang from cornices adorned with the stars of the young Republic.

In a setting of mauve and white, with green curtains and accents of purple and gold, are the works of Phyfe, McIntire, and other master cabinetmakers of New York, Boston, and Salem. Here at the table, are the chairs by Duncan Phyfe which were inherited by the mother of Mrs. Rose, Mrs. Harry Horton Benkard. These chairs were instrumental in leading Mrs. Benkard to form one of the greatest American collections.

Other examples that belonged to Mrs. Benkard are shown, along with pieces that Mr. and Mrs. Rose have collected in Europe and America. The sideboard has carving typical of Samuel McIntire of Salem. The mahogany and gilt Hepplewhite mirrors along the side wall, the Sheraton gold mirror over a distinguished New England marble-top mixing table at the end of the room, the small French Empire chandelier, the candlesticks with the early type of hurricane shades, the paintings of Canton as it appeared to Salem sea captains, all fill their appointed place in a room that perpetuates the grace and charm of the end of the eighteenth century.

THE LARKIN ADOBE
Monterey, California

Photographs: Moulin Studios

THE LIVING ROOM

Thomas O. Larkin, one of the New Englanders who went to California in the 1830's, is known to have taken New England furniture with him. However, none of the original pieces exist in the famous Monterey house that he built in 1835.

Ownership descended to Larkin's granddaughter, Mrs. H. W. Toulmin, who presented it to the National Trust. The late-eighteenth-century furniture was inherited by her from Portsmouth, New Hampshire, ancestors.

This house, like other Monterey adobes, combines Spanish colonial and New England features, but the fact that it is not built around a patio makes it rather unusual in plan. The patio is at the side, enclosed in its own walls. Here bougain-villaea, irises, and roses grow in profusion.

From 1844 to 1846 this adobe was the American consulate, and Larkin was the confidential agent of President Polk. The portrait over the fireplace is of Larkin's wife, Rachel Hobson Holmes, painted in Monterey by an unknown artist.

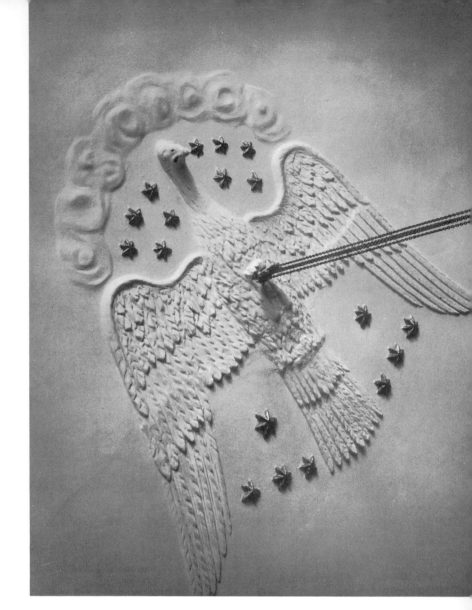

MONTICELLO

Charlottesville, Virginia

THOMAS JEFFERSON MEMORIAL FOUNDATION

THE HALL

Much is known through account books and inventories about the original furnishings of Monticello, and some of these are still in the house. Among them is the famous alcove bed, a glimpse of which, with its crimson cover fringed with yellow, can be seen from the hall. The drawing room, also entered from the hall (at right), has its original French mirrors. The folding doors of glass were there in Jefferson's time and were frequently mentioned by his visitors. The hanging lamp in the hall was brought by him from France, where he acquired furnishings which filled eighty-six cases on his return from serving as American Minister.

The hall is handsomely designed with a balustrade above; the woodwork is painted white and the walls are green. The stucco decoration on the ceiling (shown in the detail photograph) is interesting. The American eagle from the Great Seal, surrounded by stars, was a popular Federal motif, and the number of stars was sometimes accurate, sometimes a decoration without regard to the exact number at the time. In Jefferson's case it is probable that the eighteen stars on his hall ceiling record that it was finished after Louisiana, the eighteenth state, had been admitted in 1812.

THE JOHN STUART HOUSE

Charleston, South Carolina

HOME OF MR. AND MRS. JOHN D. WING

THE DRAWING ROOM

About 1772, Colonel John Stuart, who had come from England in the middle of the eighteenth century and became Commissioner of Indian Affairs, built a fine example of the Charleston "single" house, which is one room wide with a piazza at the side. Its façade has pedimented windows, an unusually rich detail in American Georgian architecture, although it is seen elsewhere in Charleston.

Photographs: Samuel Chamberlain

Color photograph: courtesy of The Ladies' Home Journal

The drawing room stretches across the entire front of the second story and is lighted by tall windows on three sides. The original paneling of this room was removed twenty years ago and is now in the Minneapolis Institute of Arts. It has, however, been replaced by an exact reproduction.

Around the mid-eighteenth century, English carpenters, masons, and joiners advertised in the South Carolina *Gazette,* many stating that they were "just arrived from London"; and it is clear from such an interior as this that English-trained workmen were available to John Stuart.

The house has known a long succession of occupants since Stuart, who was a Tory, fled from Charleston during the Revolution. Among these owners was Peter L. Gaillard, Mayor of Charleston in 1865. The present owners, Mr. and Mrs. John D. Wing, have furnished the beautiful house with equally beautiful English and French antiques.

141

Photograph: Frank Moscati

BOSCOBEL

Garrison-on-Hudson, New York

BOSCOBEL RESTORATION, INC.   THE DINING ROOM

This Hudson River country house was built in 1805 by States Morris Dyckman (1755–1806), member of an old New York family who had spent many years in England. The swagged cornice above a two-story portico, unique interpretation of the Adam style in America, may be the result of his impressions. In 1955, when demolition threatened, friends of Boscobel organized as Boscobel Restoration, Inc., with Carl Carmer as president. The house had to be moved from its original location at Crugers. The gigantic task of restoration and furnishing, after it was erected forty miles away, opposite West Point, was made possible by a generous gift from Mrs. DeWitt Wallace, member of the Restoration.

Bills for luxurious purchases by Dyckman, which still exist, provided guiding lines in selecting choice examples of English and American antiques. The Hepplewhite shield-back chairs in the dining room were made in New York about 1790. Fortunately it was possible to acquire the original Dyckman sideboard bearing a New York maker's

Photographs: Danny Wann

label, *Robart* [sic] *Wallace Joiner at the Sign of the Three Trees in Beaver Street.*
The Herculaneum dinner service on the English pedestal dining table has an urn
design and blue border.

   In the entrance hall, distinguished by its semi-elliptical arches, is a superb Moor-
fields carpet with Adam design.

VAN CORTLANDT MANOR
Croton-on-Hudson, New York

SLEEPY HOLLOW RESTORATIONS

THE PARLOR

The original fortified stone trading house at Van Cortlandt Manor was built by Stephanus, first lord of the manor, in the seventeenth century. In preparation for the occupancy of his grandson, Pierre, in 1749, it was enlarged and given the appearance which has been brought back during restoration, 1953 to 1959. Its ownership for two hundred and fifty years by the same family is possibly unparalleled among historic houses. The porch and stair are restored as they were in Pierre's time, and the round-end shingles of the roof are painted the original red. The small building was Pierre's office, from which he ruled over a domain including most of what is today Westchester County.

144

Many original furnishings are in the house, including the New York secretary and round tea table in the parlor. Marbleizing of the floor is based on the original treatment found in an adjoining passage. The paneling of the fireplace end was intact and has been given its first color, a putty shade. In the stair hall the portrait hanging over a ball-foot chest is of Pierre's brother Abraham. It is attributed to the Hudson Valley painter Pieter Vanderlyn, about 1730.

Photographs: Louis H. Frohman

GREEN PLAINS

North River, Mathews County, Virginia

HOME OF FRANCIS HIGGINSON CABOT

Photographs: Harold Haliday Costain

THE LIVING ROOM

Green Plains, built between 1798 and 1802, entered upon a new phase of existence in 1937, when it was restored by the Cabots. The estate is handsomely situated on a peninsula, and in the garden grow many examples of fine tree box and large crepe myrtles.

The large red-brick Georgian house was built by James H. Roy, son of Mungo Roy of Locust Grove, Caroline County, who married Elizabeth Booth, daughter of George Booth of Belleville, a representative in the House of Delegates (1718-1719). Additional wings were added by William H. Roy in 1838, and the window area to the right of the living room fireplace became the cupboard shown occupying this position now.

The fine antiques furnishing this room are chiefly of the late eighteenth and early nineteenth centuries. A round Aubusson rug has a floral design in soft colors echoed in the rest of the room, and the Directoire couch with delicate brass inlay is an unusually beautiful adaptation of a classic form.

Photographs: Harold Haliday Costain

ALMODINGTON
Near Oriole, Maryland
A HOME IN SOMERSET COUNTY

THE LIVING ROOM

The small panes of glass in an eighteenth-century window divide an inviting view of Almodington's parlor into a checkerboard of fascinating details showing late eighteenth-century French and English furnishings in a mid-eighteenth-century colonial setting.

Almodington, on the eastern shore of Chesapeake Bay in the Manokin River district, belonged to the distinguished Elzey family of Maryland, who owned 1000 acres of land here in 1663. The house was built around 1750, probably by Arnold E. Elzey, and was later the home of James Elzey, one of Washington's officers in the Battle of Long Island. Original paneling from Almodington is now in the American Wing of the Metropolitan Museum. The house is an interesting one as a rural interpretation of urban architecture, found so often in the South. Native yellow pine, the "hard" pine of the South, was used in paneling the walls and for the floors as well. The exterior is distinguished by the use of brickwork in the Flemish bond; window arches of gauged, or shaped, brick; as well as a belt course to mark the second story.

The furnishings here represent the taste of a modern collector, who has chosen English pieces of the Adam period to accompany Louis XV and Louis XVI chairs in a room that has formality as well as simplicity.

HOUSE IN MILWAUKEE
Wisconsin

HOME OF MR. AND MRS. STANLEY STONE

THE DINING ROOM

Through the molded arch in the hall is an attractive first glimpse of the dining room and a Salem butler's secretary. In the view of the whole room, the unusually ornamental secretary, with painted glass panels in white and gold below the glazed doors and an eagle finial above, is seen at closer range.

Photographs: Taylor & Dull

The American furniture collected by Mr. and Mrs. Stone is of an exceptional quality, their taste inclining to Chippendale but turning to Sheraton and Hepplewhite for the dining room. The sideboard with serpentine front was made in New York or New Jersey. The Hepplewhite shield-back chairs show the carved basket-of-fruit motif at the top of the cresting rail which justifies an attribution to Samuel McIntire of Salem. They are covered in cut velvet with a pattern in dark red on a gold ground.

A choice collection of porcelain including Chinese "Lowestoft" porcelain is displayed in the dining room cabinet. This ware is now being called China-Trade porcelain by students, for it was made for export and filled the holds of ships engaged in the China trade. The cabinet, one of a pair, is painted, like the rest of the room, an aquamarine blue, with a delicate pink in the shell.

The house, designed in traditional Georgian style by Andrew H. Hepburn of the Boston firm of Perry, Shaw & Hepburn, was built as a setting for antiques.

HOUSE IN SCARBOROUGH
New York

HOME OF MRS. GILES WHITING

THE PORCELAIN ROOM

In a small room adjoining the dining room of her Hudson River home, Mrs. Whiting has arranged some of her English porcelain figures and many examples of lusterware. The room is also notable for the attractive selection and grouping of American Hepplewhite and Sheraton furniture. A New England Queen Anne tea table, displaying a luster tea set, stands in front of a Martha Washington chair.

A Chelsea shepherd and shepherdess stand on a Sheraton inlaid desk attributed to John Seymour of Boston. Over the desk is a Bilbao mirror, its elaborate crest in pristine state. This rare Hepplewhite type was brought in American ships from Bilbao, Spain, although it was probably made elsewhere in Europe.

Beyond the fireplace stands a Baltimore folding-top card table with inlaid stringing of satinwood and small ovals stained green. A single bellflower suspended like a tassel on all four legs is indicative of Baltimore.

The color in the room is dominated by a contrast of the pale sage green of the walls and the golden yellow of the antique damask draperies and sofa cover. The rug is yellow and the chairs are upholstered in a light, subtle green. The woodwork is antique white.

The house, built at nearby Sleepy Hollow about 1830-1840 and moved to its present location in 1861, is a rare survival of Greek Revival architecture in the lower Hudson Valley.

Photograph: Bender

Photograph: Samuel Chamberlain

Photograph: Taylor & Dull

ASA STEBBINS HOUSE

Deerfield, Massachusetts

HERITAGE FOUNDATION

THE NORTH PARLOR

Blue-green walls, white woodwork, and looped-back curtains of cherry-red satin make a colorful setting for the American Sheraton and Hepplewhite furniture. The Aubusson rug of beige, rose, and green repeats the same colors in lighter tones.

The English luster chandelier, made about 1770-1785, is one of the much-sought examples in small size. New York square-back Sheraton side chairs, after a design in Sheraton's *Drawing Book,* a Salem card table inlaid in patterned satinwood, and a small drop-leaf table (set with decanter and wineglasses), represent an aristocratic period in American furniture making, 1790-1800.

Among the accessories in the parlor (including a collection of porcelain and glass in a wall cabinet next the fireplace) is the little portrait medallion of Franklin, a cameo incrustation in glass, probably made in France. The house was remodeled in 1790 and, as furnished now, represents Federal New England at its best.

Photograph: Taylor & Dull

HAMMOND-HARWOOD HOUSE

Annapolis, Maryland

HAMMOND-HARWOOD HOUSE ASSOCIATION

THE DINING ROOM

In the year 1774, when the new home of Matthias Hammond, wealthy Annapolis barrister and patriot, was reaching completion, the owner himself was deeply involved in the chaotic events preceding the Revolution. He was a member of the General Convention of 1774 and of the committee which sanctioned the burning of the brigantine *Peggy Stewart,* with her cargo of the hated, taxed tea, in Chesapeake Bay.

The architect of the house, William Buckland, died in 1774, having created the masterpiece of his career, begun so brilliantly at Gunston Hall (page 82). His final exposition of the Palladian style shows rococo influence in the naturalistic floral garlands over the fanlight of the entrance door. Within, there is a wealth of finely carved detail, rich cornices, scrolled pediments, and paneled chimney breasts.

The house, where Hammond lived as a bachelor after being jilted by the young lady for whom he intended it, passed by inheritance to the Harwood family. In the dining room the Chippendale chairs and Hepplewhite sideboard and table are from this family. Portraits of Buckland's wife and children by Charles Willson Peale also hang in this room. The ballroom has an English Broadwood piano and Adam chairs. In the ladies' parlor is a rare Baltimore Hepplewhite breakfront bookcase with the inlaid ovals often seen in Baltimore work.

Photographs: Louis H. Frohman

THE WILLIAM GIBBES HOUSE
Charleston, South Carolina

HOME OF MR. AND MRS. ASHBY FARROW

Photographs: Samuel Chamberlain

THE BALLROOM

The second-floor ballroom of the William Gibbes house presents a dazzling effect. This is achieved not only with the great chandelier and its spraylike canopy, but with the richness of the Adam decoration which was added to the Georgian interior at the beginning of the nineteenth century. One can readily imagine whirling crinolines and coattails during antebellum balls in this room of yellow and gold.

The plasterwork on the ceiling, an elaborate Adam mantel with stucco festoons, and the neoclassic ornament on the door frames represent a fine type of Charleston stucco work, the evidence of increasing prosperity of South Carolina planters just after the turn of the century, when so many of these houses were redecorated.

French furnishings here include a Louis XVI sofa and armchair and Louis XV side chairs, which have their original light blue paint. The Aubusson rug has a deep ivory ground on which the gold scrollwork produces a luminous effect. A Chinese Chippendale mirror negates the laws of symmetry seen in the chaste classic ornament on the door frame.

The Gibbes house, one of the handsomest of Charleston's double houses, was built about 1779 when the merchant owner had his own wharf opposite, running out into the Ashley River.

Photographs: Samuel Chamberlain

THE DRAWING ROOM

An early Charleston drawing room is to be seen in the Thomas Rose house, built around 1735. Unlike most houses in Charleston, it has suffered little change in a city in which war, flood, hurricane, and earthquake have wrought great damage to property in the past.

The original plan of the house is unaltered, and the old paneling remains intact. The fine Adam mantel, however, was added later and is typical of the "modernization" of so many Charleston homes about 1800.

In this gracious Georgian setting are appropriate English Chippendale and Hepplewhite furniture, Chinese porcelains, French ormolu, English and Continental enamels. The portrait hanging above the fireplace is by John Berridge, a pupil of Sir Joshua Reynolds.

The golden-yellow draperies, with tapering side panels and festoons above, are in the Adam manner and so disposed that they accentuate rather than obscure the paneling of the deep window recesses. Walls and ceiling are painted a soft beige-yellow which complements the deeper yellows, golds, and whites featured in the furnishings and accessories.

WICKHAM-VALENTINE HOUSE

Richmond, Virginia

THE VALENTINE MUSEUM

THE SMALL PARLOR

In what Hamlin's *Greek Revival Architecture* calls "one of the most formally simple yet elegant houses of the general 'Regency' type," this parlor exemplifies Robert Mills's imaginative treatment of the neoclassic.

That Mills was the architect of the Wickham-Valentine House is generally conceded, although there is no actual record. Other similar work, known to be his, is seen elsewhere in Richmond on Church Hill.

Photographs: Dementi

The parlor is entered from an oval hall, the doorway of which shows a free rendering of the Doric order. Doubtless the architect intended that the wall niche should hold a piece of classic sculpture. The parlor has recently been restored to its original paint treatment with gilding applied to the narrow moldings and the raised ornament on the mantel frieze and door frames. The background is a delicate gray-white. Windows are hung with lampas draperies in the Federal style.

The overdoor panels, now dimmed in color, take their design from Flaxman's illustrations for the *Iliad*, published in 1805. The Sheraton armchair at the right once belonged to Dolly Madison (or Dolley, as she signed herself).

HARRISON GRAY OTIS HOUSE

Boston, Massachusetts

SOCIETY FOR THE PRESERVATION OF NEW ENGLAND ANTIQUITIES

THE DINING ROOM

After the Boston architect Charles Bulfinch visited England and made the Grand Tour of the Continent in the 1780's he brought a knowledge of current developments in Europe to America.

In domestic architecture this house, built in 1795 from a design that has been traced to Bulfinch, is an excellent example of the neoclassic style new to America

164

at the time. The style was destined to sweep the Atlantic coast in the next two decades, until it in turn was supplanted by a fresh wave of classicism known as the Greek Revival.

The mantel in the dining room with a medallion showing the Triumph of a Roman Emperor has the purity of a design by Flaxman, and all the Adam ornament here has a close resemblance to its English prototype.

The dado and panels on the doors are a light pastel green, used with white that runs to cream color. The portrait of an unknown gentleman over the fireplace, attributed to John Greenwood, shows a view of Boston in the background. Argand lamps stand on either side of the mantel.

Photographs: Samuel Chamberlain

THE PEIRCE-NICHOLS HOUSE

Salem, Massachusetts

THE ESSEX INSTITUTE

THE SOUTHEAST CHAMBER

The hand of Samuel McIntire, the architect and wood-carver of Salem, is doubly evident here. Not only is this house the best-known of his many Salem houses, but here in this bedroom with its pretty, bright blue wallpaper, the Sheraton bed with carved and reeded posts shows his handiwork in the carved ornament. The bed is one of many pieces original to the house, and the printed cotton hangings on it have a design in brown on a light beige ground. The Massachusetts block-front chest-on-chest near the door is of the finest quality.

Architecturally, the house is interesting for McIntire's fully developed neoclassic style in the remodeled east parlor of 1801, and in the hall and in the chamber above it. Additionally, the original part of the house shows what is in all probability McIntire's early manner, although no definite attribution can be made.

Jerathmiel Peirce purchased the property on Federal Street in 1779, and the house, a fine late Georgian mansion, was built by 1782. It was remodeled by McIntire at the time of the marriage of Peirce's daughter, Sally, to George Nichols, and the house later became their home.

166

PONT READING

Ardmore, Pennsylvania

HOME OF MR. AND MRS. DAVID B. ROBB

Engraving by A. Bowen after William Lynn.

THE STAIR HALL

The beautiful honey-colored maple used in this stairway, the double entrance doors, and the doors to the library and parlor at either side, was cut on the place and seasoned in the shipbuilding yards of its owner. He was our first naval constructor, Joshua Humphreys, designer of the U. S. Frigate *Constitution* and sister ships, the *Constellation, Congress, President,* and *United States.*

Humphreys enlarged his family home in 1813. The eighteenth-century section (center and rear) still incorporates logs from the much older, seventeenth-century house built by the founder of the family in America, Daniel Humphreys. The dormers are a mid-nineteenth-century addition.

The designation Pont Reading appears in records as early as 1785 and is said to have been the name of the family home in Wales. The house has remained continuously in the family except for the period 1932-1948, and when purchased in 1948 by the Robbs came back into its possession, as Mrs. Robb is a direct descendant of Daniel Humphreys. Since both Mr. and Mrs. Robb have inherited Philadelphia and New Jersey Queen Anne and Chippendale furniture, the house has become virtually a museum. Among a number of great examples of Chippendale furniture is a pair of "ribbon back" side chairs, which stand in the hall. One is shown in the detail photograph. These chairs, probably made in Pennsylvania or in New Jersey, were inherited by Mr. Robb from the Haines family of New Jersey.

Photographs: Charles Mills & Sons

HOUSE IN JACONA
New Mexico

THE DINING ROOM

Hitchcock chairs with original stenciling, a drop-leaf table from Cape Cod, a New England banjo clock, early pine dresser, and a New England earthenware jug are among the furnishings in a house which shows a tasteful combination of antiques from New England with Mexican and Indian art. The parlor has paneling from Cape Cod, the sitting room is papered (wallpaper was used in New Mexico after about 1850), but the dining room is New Mexican, with original ceiling of typical round beams and a corner fireplace.

Mexican silver candlesticks, tin chandelier, and the mirror and tin sconce by the fireplace are all of southwestern origin. The figure of a saint, or *bulto,* over the fireplace is one of a large collection of *bultos* and *santos,* many of which their owner

Photographs: Tyler Dingee

has lent to the Museum of New Mexico in Santa Fe. These primitives of the south-west face, quite harmoniously, the "Flow Blue" Staffordshire in the same room.

John Gaw Meem was the architect for this Spanish colonial type house built around two original adobes.

171

LEMON HILL
Philadelphia, Pennsylvania

COLONIAL DAMES OF AMERICA, CHAPTER II

THE PARLOR

Lemon Hill in Fairmount Park was opened to the public at the end of 1957. In its oval parlor is a justly famous set of Louis XVI furniture that has a long history of ownership in Philadelphia.

The sofa and twelve armchairs still have their original pale greenish-white paint with gold decoration but have been re-covered in modern lampas of eighteenth-

Photographs: courtesy of the Philadelphia Museum of Art

century pattern. The set belonged in the eighteenth century to Edward Burd and then to his son, Edward Shippen Burd. The pure French design and fine workmanship gradually caused them to be considered French and even attached to them the tradition that they had "belonged to Marie Antoinette." Their appearance at auction in New York in 1921 eventually led to a discovery of their true identity as Philadelphia masterpieces of chairmaking. They passed through the sale room without question, and it was only when they were sent to France and their Beauvais coverings removed that the American framework was discovered. They returned,

minus the Beauvais, and were purchased in 1929 by Fiske Kimball, who used them here while residing at Lemon Hill.

The walls of this room are cream color, the woodwork being a dark gray-blue with mahogany doors. The rose-colored curtains are silk damask in an Empire pattern.

The first lemon trees in Philadelphia were grown on this estate, and thus the name Lemon Hill came into existance. There is some doubt about the origin of the house, but it may have been built, or remodeled, about 1798 by Henry Pratt.

HOUSE IN RITTENHOUSE SQUARE
Philadelphia, Pennsylvania

HOME OF HENRY P. MCILHENNY

THE DRAWING ROOM

174

These views of a room in Mr. McIlhenny's Philadelphia house show a predominantly French Directoire and Empire theme.

The French mood provides a perfect background for Ingres' *Portrait of the Comtesse de Tournon* over the mantel, and allows for a shift in period with Renoir's impressionist *Portrait of Mlle. Legrand,* which hangs over the exceptionally fine Empire Amboina wood and ormolu commode. Other famous works of art seen in these views include Toulouse-Lautrec's large canvas, *Moulin Rouge—The Dance,* over the side table and a Degas sculpture in the corner near the fireplace.

Mr. McIlhenny is curator of decorative arts at the Philadelphia Museum of Art. Apart from his magnificent collection of paintings on his own walls, he has a notable collection of English, French, and American furniture, silver, and porcelain.

THE PARLOR

Built in 1815, the Culver House is the oldest in Rochester. Oliver Culver, a surveyor who came from Connecticut to this area in 1797, when it was little more than a wilderness, first built in 1805 a story-and-a-half house which he later remodeled, in

the Federal neoclassic manner, with pedimented entrance. The slenderness, symmetry, and restraint with which American builders and house carpenters designed in this idiom is evident throughout the house and is seen here in the well-proportioned parlor mantelpiece with its pairs of free-standing colonnettes.

The present owner has brought together many antiques which have descended in Rochester families, including Hepplewhite shield-back side chairs. The overmantel mirror, with columns, is typical of the Federal style about 1810.

Delicate shades of eggshell, citron green, and coral are used throughout the room against the warm eggshell pink walls and self-striped silk hangings which are lined with a small-patterned chintz. The circular Aubusson rug is pale green with a floral design of lilacs, roses, tulips, and dahlias.

177

THE OWENS-THOMAS HOUSE 1816
Savannah, Georgia
THE TELFAIR ACADEMY

Photographs: Andrew Bunn

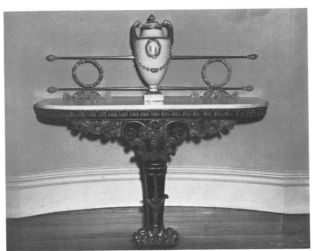

178

THE NORTHWEST DRAWING ROOM

The young English architect, William Jay, left his stamp on Savannah, and there is nothing quite like his work in other cities. It is often compared to English Regency but could also be called a very personal and free expression of Adam's classicism, more airy in effect, with old motifs considerably magnified and used boldly, as seen here in the palmette and festoon cornice.

The walls of the room are blue, and the mauve and gold draperies frame black settees ornamented with gold. The Regency glass sconces on either side of the fireplace, perfect examples of their period, are of a set of four in the room, and the brass fender with Regency motifs broadly spaced is exceptionally handsome.

The introduction of Hepplewhite and Sheraton chairs of fine quality at the fireplace saves the room from being too monotonously "in period." The mahogany and marble console with brass gallery was apparently part of the original furnishings and possibly came from Europe, an example of late Empire or of the transition style which is beginning to be called William IV. The large scale of the acanthus, the scrolls and paw foot shows the trend of the time toward heavier forms.

179

BARTOW MANSION

Pelham Bay, New York

THE INTERNATIONAL GARDEN CLUB

Photographs: Gottscho-Schleisner

THE PARLOR

Empire furniture in the architectural setting of a Greek Revival house is seen at Bartow, a house attributed to the New York architect Minard Lafever.

In the parlor, neoclassic detail, such as the large-scale anthemion, is combined with the eagle motif on the window pediments, an emblem typical of the Federal period. The Empire rosewood piano is signed *John Geib & Sons New York;* and the bronze and cut-glass oil lamp which stands on it, a type used in the 1830's, is marked *P Gardiner N.York.*

The walls of the room are a pale reddish brown, the floors black, the woodwork white, the doors mahogany—producing bold notes of color that emphasize the symmetry of the plan. The draperies, based on designs taken from a work published in London in 1826 by George Smith, are copper and robin's-egg blue, repeating the more subdued colors in the Savonnerie carpet of the Charles X period. Beyond the parlor is the dining room (see opposite), entered through so wide a door that the two rooms are united, and the same colors have been used there, but with minor variations. The chandeliers in both rooms, with their hurricane shades and cut prisms, are fine examples of about 1810.

Photographs: Cortlandt V. D. Hubbard

ANDALUSIA
Bucks County, Pennsylvania
HOME OF CHARLES J. BIDDLE

THE WEST YELLOW PARLOR

No home in America is more closely associated with its early owner than is Andalusia with Nicholas Biddle, president of the Second Bank of America, implacable foe of Jackson, and more instrumental even than the Greek Revival architects in making Philadelphia the "Athens of America." Andalusia is now in the possession of the grandson, Charles J. Biddle.

The Doric peristyle on the south front is the great example of Greek temple architecture adapted to the American mansion. This part of the house, designed by Thomas U. Walter, was added about 1830 to an already existing, and notable, Federal house built in 1795 by Mrs. Biddle's father, John Craig.

Walter's addition on the front facing the Delaware River joined the original structure in such a way that the new or West Yellow Parlor was approached through the windows of the old, or Regency, parlor, as seen from the hall in the view above.

From the West Yellow Parlor, the East Yellow Parlor is entered through sliding doors. The two rooms are virtually one, and their handsome fireplaces have similar white and gold mirrors with carved palmettes, husks, urns, and paterae. The white marble mantels were brought from Italy.

The great bronze and water-gilt chandeliers, in themselves an epitome of classic ornament, came from France.

Photographs: Harold Haliday Costain

BELLINGRATH GARDENS

Theodore, Alabama

BELLINGRATH FOUNDATION

THE DRAWING ROOM

The possibilities offered by a room of spacious proportions for a mingling of periods and styles in a harmonious whole are again especially well realized here.

The Adam mantel, eighteenth-century chandelier, and an eighteenth-century tea table are shown with Empire and early Victorian furniture in well-balanced relationship.

The grillwork in the court of Bellingrath Gardens makes effective use of the nineteenth-century ornamental ironwork so distinctively and romantically associated with Southern architecture.

The handsome hallway (illustrated above) leads into the living room where we see authentic eighteenth- and nineteenth-century styles freely mixed.

The house and the famous gardens created by Mr. and Mrs. Walter D. Bellingrath are now open to the public under the care of the Foundation.

Photographs: *Harold Haliday Costain*

THE DRAWING ROOM

The charm of Early Victorian while it was dominated by the Louis Philippe style of France is seen in this Natchez drawing room.

Since Arlington was built for Jane Surget White, daughter of Pierre Surget who came to Natchez from France in the early nineteenth century, French taste has been a family inheritance.

The columned porch of Arlington is that of the Greek temple style used all over America in the early part of the nineteenth century but with particular flair in the South.

In the drawing room, the great French chandelier with its sparkling prisms, the gilt overmantel mirrors, the Louis Philippe sofas and chairs with delicately carved backs represent a period, the second quarter of the nineteenth century, of which few examples so pure as this survive.

The walls of the room are covered with French hand-blocked paper in gold and white designs, and the furniture and draperies are tailored in yellow satin brocade. Touches of dark wine and Sèvres royal blue are worked into the design of the beige Aubusson carpet.

In certain exterior details the architecture is that of houses built along the Atlantic coast about 1810. Within a decade such a fanlight as is seen above over the entrance door was introduced in the Mississippi Valley.

MELROSE

Natchez, Mississippi

HOME OF MRS. GEORGE MALIN DAVIS KELLY

Photographs: Harold Haliday Costain

THE PARLOR

Surrounded by its boxwood gardens, Melrose is one of the sights of the countryside near Natchez. It was built in 1845 by Judge Edward Turner for his daughter
and is thus a contemporary of the Governor's Mansion at Jackson, a famous example
of the Greek Revival style designed by William Nichols in 1842 which greatly influenced Mississippi architecture.

After the War between the States Melrose was purchased by George Malin Davis
and has descended in his family. The interior woodwork, as seen from the hall,
shows classic details; but the furniture is Victorian at its height, each piece having
richly carved floral crests in the Belter style.

At the right of the fireplace is a "courting set," an ingenious variant of a Victorian
double-chair love seat, which provided the chaperon with a place to sit between her
charges. The handsome chandelier, with its lamp globes and chimneys, is a rare
survival of nineteenth-century lighting in the grand manner.

The two connecting parlors have sunny yellow walls. Green and gold are used
in the front parlor in both the brocatelle draperies and furniture upholstery, while
a pink and gold color scheme is featured in the room shown.

188

THE LIBRARY AND PARLOR

Victorian furnishings in a house which, when it was built in 1855, embodied perfectly the romantic ideal of a gentleman's rural retreat, have survived here in a rare state of preservation. The house, in modified Italian villa style, is of rose-red brick trimmed with limestone and has an end tower, coupled windows, and canopied verandah. It was designed by the New York architect, Gervase Wheeler, shortly after he had published *Rural Homes,* and was built for Patrick Barry, who in 1840 became the partner of George Ellwanger. Their Mount Hope Botanical and Pomological Gardens

Photographs: Lodder

was the most notable of all American nurseries and their magnificent horticultural library is now on loan at the University of Rochester.

The parlor and library, which adjoin, received new draperies in 1886. An invoice for them from a New York firm in November of that year is in the possession of Mr. Frederick Barry, the present owner of the house. The draperies in the parlor are a deep aquamarine silk plush with an unusually long pile and are heavily fringed. They hang from a valance board of rosewood or mahogany with a goldleaf, carved initial "B" in the center. The rosewood furniture was reupholstered at the same time in aquamarine and silver brocade. A Wilton wall-to-wall carpet has a golden yellow ground with a self-pattern of scrolling. The carpet color repeats the wall color, a strong yellow-gold, and the woodwork is a light stone color. Doors are beautifully grained to simulate mahogany. The library, which can be seen from the parlor, has the same wall and woodwork treatment, with hangings of golden brown silk plush and upholstery of golden brown brocatelle. An extant, better-documented Victorian interior would be difficult to find, although it may be at variance with our present conception of a beautiful interior.

191

BELLE MEADE

Nashville, Tennessee

THE ASSOCIATION FOR THE PRESERVATION OF TENNESSEE ANTIQUITIES

THE PARLOR

The Victorian period's imitation of many styles, including Gothic, French, Elizabethan, and numerous others, was halted at mid-nineteenth century by its most nearly original expression. The parlor at Belle Meade in Nashville is a handsome example of this.

It was at mid-century that the cabinetmaker John Belter of New York trailed his heavily carved grapevines across the backs of chairs and sofas and draped his oval tables with pierced friezes that barely permitted a view of the fruit and flower finials on the cross-stretchers below. Belter's work is well represented in this crimson, black, and gold parlor. Twin fireplaces and a broad cornice are important features of the room. The architect of Belle Mead was William Strickland, who worked extensively in the South.

The house was built for Giles Harding; and all of the materials including Tennessee limestone as well as the walnut, cherry, oak, and ash used in the interior came from his own five-hundred-acre estate. Belle Meade was well known for its nursery of thoroughbred horses established by Harding, the first in the United States. This fourteen-room mansion, which has recently been acquired by the State of Tennessee, has survived many of its neighbors and well represents the grandeur of 1850.

193

HOUSE IN SUTTON SQUARE

New York City

HOME OF MR. AND MRS. NORMAN K. WINSTON

Photographs: Jerome Zerbe

THE DRAWING ROOM

With this house in Sutton Square, New York, there is introduced here a brief review of traditional styles used in rooms with modern feeling. In the Winston drawing room paintings by modern French masters create such an effect inevitably. The point to be noted is that eighteenth-century French furniture and porcelains accompany them harmoniously.

Most of the furniture in the Winstons' home is French of the periods of Louis XV and Louis XVI. The French flair for ornament in ormolu-mounted and inlaid pieces is balanced by French restraint in the use of off-white painted furniture. In this carefully considered setting, where there is neither too much nor too little of the *ancien régime,* there has been introduced with striking effect one of the great "little" collections of nineteenth-century French masters from Delacroix to Degas, chiefly paintings small in scale. These and more modern works by Picasso, Matisse and others, assembled with great taste over a number of years, are highly appreciated by the art critics, and that they appear to perfect advantage with the French decorative arts created for the period of Pompadour and Marie Antoinette is obvious from these photographs. French eighteenth-century porcelains, terra cottas, and embroideries, French silver, and Savonnerie carpets adorn the house without distracting attention from its great treasure, a significant collection of modern French paintings.

HOUSE IN HARFORD COUNTY
Maryland

HOME OF HARVEY LADEW

THE LIBRARY

Remodeling an old Maryland house has given Harvey Ladew an opportunity to introduce his noteworthy collection of English furniture, porcelains, and paintings in a setting which has been designed for them, and for modern living as well. The house is situated in rolling countryside that is admirably suited to his interest in fox hunting. His large oval library is greatly admired. The oval form was a favorite one with early nineteenth-century architects, but is developed here on larger than usual scale, and with modern simplicity of interior design. The fine proportions of the Chippendale oval library table, a great piece of English cabinetmaking, are emphasized by the room itself. The Georgian mantel of green and white Irish marble supports an eighteenth-century English bracket clock. At the window (left) is a Sheraton semicircular hunt table, devised for serving a huntsman's repast. Through the richly carved eighteenth-century doorway at the end of the room is a view of the oak-paneled Elizabethan room.

197

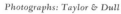

Photographs: Taylor & Dull

TOWN HOUSE
New York City

HOME OF MR. AND MRS. CHARLES C. PATERSON

THE DRAWING ROOM

The new manner in which tapestries are arranged is an all-important feature of this New York City drawing room. Where in former years tapestries hung in close proximity on dark, paneled walls, here they are widely spaced on plain wall surfaces (pale celadon in tone) with the result that their own fine colors appear to float in the clear light.

Louis XV and Louis XVI carved *bergères* and *fauteuils* are used with severely simple mahogany tables decorated only with delicate metal galleries. Among subdued notes of color furnished by porcelains and embroideries, a pleasing contribution comes from the polychrome frieze of a great English Tudor draw table of oak.

The English Regency chandelier with plumelike branches, designed with an understanding of that timeless "line of beauty," the curve, is very much in keeping with the rest of the furnishings. Throughout this room the importance of line has been well understood.

198

HOUSE IN LOS ANGELES
California

HOME OF MR. AND MRS. HAROLD C. RAMSER

THE DINING ROOM

In this modern home in California there is a happy blending of new and old. The dining room has antique furniture, chiefly English, and an eighteenth-century corner cupboard (open to display a notable collection of English silver) which came from the Middle States, possibly Maryland. The mirror wall at its left is thoroughly modern, but the antique chandelier which it reflects is used as originally intended, with candles.

The graceful silver epergne on the table is by Thomas Pennell, London, 1764, and is accompanied by candlesticks by Paul Storr. The handsome kettle on the top shelf of the cupboard (shown also in detail) is the work of William Shaw and William Priest in the year George III became king.

On the bottom shelf of the cupboard is a pair of double-lipped sauce boats. These, by Thomas Gilpin, London, 1744, follow a French form brought over by the Huguenot silversmiths. The cupboard also shows a set of four George III tureens by John Parker, 1803, with the arms of Lonsdale.

200

Photographs: Harold Haliday Costain

THE DRAWING ROOM

The art of arranging a great collection of porcelain in a modern home without turning it into a museum is well understood by Mr. and Mrs. Meloney, who have assembled the most important collection of French soft paste in America and introduced it quite informally in their home at Riverdale. Informality and a modern touch also characterize the treatment of the chimneybreast with mirror panel in today's style, but emphasis returns to the past with the fine Chippendale carved swag used as an overmantel decoration.

Among porcelains unique in the strict sense of that abused term is the Chantilly white porcelain bust of Louis XV on the Adam console table at the right, while the Mennecy portrait of that same royal patron of porcelain (Adam console, left) is elsewhere known only among the Morgan porcelains in Hartford. The Hepplewhite satinwood cabinet (it was once owned by Lord Leverhulme) contains unique Mennecy pieces, a *Vendeur* in white and a polychrome pair of *Mendiants*. On the Chippendale pedestal table is a Chantilly parrot. Hepplewhite furniture "in the French taste" includes barrel-back chairs, rare in the Hepplewhite style. White coverings accord with a high-keyed color scheme. Curtains are pale gold and the antique Kuba rug is dominated by faded pinks and blues. The Dufour wallpaper in the "Bay of Naples" pattern is printed in sepia and cream. At the left of the window is a very rare inlaid satinwood lace box on a stand, representing English cabinetmaking of utmost refinement.

202

Photographs: Wendy Hilty

HOUSE IN SAN ANTONIO

Texas

HOME OF MR. AND MRS. LUTCHER BROWN

THE LIVING ROOM

In this Texas living room there is seen an understanding of the use of antiques to secure the livable air without which any room, no matter how fine its components, must be counted a failure.

The magnificent house, without and within, has been designed with respect for tradition, but it is a modern house and its antiques are used in modern taste. The high-ceilinged living room, which has a wide cornice and overdoor panels in relief, offers the challenge of a great amount of space in which to maintain the casual, unstudied air we like today. The use of large landscape panels which introduce the glowing colors of nature into this white setting has warded off any coldness that might be felt in a room of these proportions.

Choice of Hepplewhite and Sheraton furniture has been a wise one. These pieces are distinguished in line and are light, have the virtue of being easily moved and seem to have the ability of arranging themselves in chance but effective groupings. They lend themselves, too, to the planned vista, as where a Hepplewhite sofa covered in striped silk is seen from the paneled library.

204

Photographs: Harold Haliday Costain

Charles Fairchild Fuller, architect

CROWFIELDS

Mt. Kisco, New York

HOME OF CASS CANFIELD

THE HALL

The green hall in Cass Canfield's modern home at Mt. Kisco has Adam details as well as later expressions of neoclassic design interpreted with today's simplicity.

Robert Adam, when not overly concerned with overly elaborate detail, was quite capable of showing his appreciation of the beauty of cylinders, prisms, and cubes. There is, besides, something modern in the style of any age the moment it employs plain surfaces and clean-cut lines. The wall surfaces, the furniture, the decorations here do not depart from simplicity; and the combination of Adam, Directoire, and Empire furnishings allows no undue emphasis on any one style. The American banjo clock is but one element of many lending emphasis to geometric forms in this unusually handsome hallway.

In 1753 Hogarth wrote: "The moderns have carried simplicity, convenience and neatness of workmanship to a very high degree of perfection"; and the "moderns" of today have done the same, by the very use they make of the arts of the past.

206

THE LIVING ROOM

Thoroughly modern in feeling is the manner in which a large-scale eighteenth-century Bolognese painting of classic architecture is used as a wall decoration in this living room. The arts of eighteenth-century Italy predominate here, but French and modern pieces are used also. The manner of arrangement only seems casual; actually the relationship of each piece to the rest has been carefully considered so that from every angle the room shows good design.

The Italian eighteenth-century sofa and armchairs, painted blue and gold, are up-holstered in white linen, while the cushions on the sofa are covered in Florentine silk with a floral pattern after Botticelli. On either side are Neapolitan eighteenth-century console tables in silver, gray, and white. The old gilt tôle sconces above them are de-signed as tall urns of flowers and have candle arms in floral form.

The walls of the room are pearl gray, and a gray Fortuny fabric covers the Louis XV chair which is drawn up at a low circular marble-topped table, as seen in the view on the opposite page. The large sofa, which stands in front of a handsome pair of torchères in the form of blackamoors, is covered in green damask. An Aubusson carpet has a pastel blue and rose flower design on a pale gold ground.

HOUSE ON LONG ISLAND
Locust Valley, New York

HOME OF MR. AND MRS. RENZO OLIVIERI

Photographs: Wendy Hilty

Acknowledgments

I AM DEEPLY GRATEFUL TO ALICE WINCHESTER, EDITOR OF *Antiques,* for the encouragement and help she has given me in the preparation of this book. Specifically, I am indebted for permission to draw on material in the department Living with Antiques for the Ogden house in Connecticut, Time Stone Farm in Massachusetts, Andelys and Mowbra Hall in New York, Pont Reading in Pennsylvania, Longago and Mount Cuba in Delaware, The Lindens in Washington, D. C., and Filoli, La Pineta, and the Larkin Adobe in California. Other homes from that department include the New York town house of Mr. and Mrs. Charles C. Paterson, the Connecticut home of Mr. and Mrs. Frederic C. Peck, the house of Mr. and Mrs. Harold C. Ramser in Los Angeles, the Long Island residence of Mr. and Mrs. Reginald P. Rose, and the homes of Mrs. J. Stogdell Stokes in Bryn Mawr, Mr. and Mrs. Stanley Stone in Milwaukee, Mr. and Mrs. Mitchel Taradash at Ardsley-on-Hudson, and Mrs. Giles Whiting at Scarborough, New York. In my presentation of historic houses I have drawn upon *Antiques* for the Saugus Iron-master's house and Parson Ashley house in Massachusetts; the Buttolph-Williams house in Connecticut; Schuyler Mansion and the Van Cortlandt house in New York; Marlpit Hall and William Trent house in New Jersey; Mount Vernon, Gunston Hall, Stratford, and the Wickham-Valentine house in Virginia. I wish also to acknowledge indebtedness to contributors: Harold Donaldson Eberlein and C. V. D. Hubbard for Andalusia; John A. H. Sweeney for Corbit House, and E. Boyd for the Jacona home of H. Cady Wells.

I am indebted to *Town & Country* for material on Drayton in Maryland; Green Plains and The Horseshoe in Virginia; Boxwood and Mimosa Hall in Georgia, as well as the New York City house of Mr. and Mrs. Norman K. Winston and the Maryland home of Harvey Ladew.

The state chapters of the National Society of Colonial Dames of America in Connecticut, New York, and Virginia have been helpful in supplying information, and other organizations which have kindly aided are the Society for the Preservation of New England Antiquities, Colonial Williamsburg, and the Essex Institute. I also thank, for suggestions and help, William Baldwin, Miss Emily Davie, Mrs. Clement Griffin, Miss Elizabeth Holahan, and Mrs. Sifford Pearre.

For three color illustrations I acknowledge the courtesy of the Henry Francis du Pont Winterthur Museum and The Macmillan Company. My thanks also to Richard and Dorothy Pratt for three color photographs taken under their supervision and to *Life* Magazine for the photographs by Arnold Newman. And last but not least, my heartfelt thanks to the owners of the houses.